PAINTBALL
AND AIRSOFT
BATTLE TACTICS

Christopher E. Larsen
Photography by Hae-jung Larsen
Schematics by John T. Gordon

Voyageur Press

First published in 2008 by Voyageur Press, an imprint of MBI Publishing Company, 400 First Avenue North, Suite 300, Minneapolis, MN 55401 USA

Voyageur Press titles are also available at discounts in bulk quantity for industrial or sales-promotional use. For details write to Special Sales Manager at MBI Publishing Company, 400 First Avenue North, Suite 300, Minneapolis, MN 55401 USA

To find out more about our books, join us online at www.voyageurpress.com.

Library of Congress Cataloging-in-Publication Data

Larsen, Christopher E., 1967-
  Paintball and airsoft battle tactics / text by Christopher E. Larsen ; photography by Hae-jung Larsen ; schematics by John T. Gordon.
    p. cm.
  ISBN-13: 978-0-7603-3063-0 (softbound)
  ISBN-10: 0-7603-3063-8 (softbound)
  1. Paintball (Game)—Handbooks, manuals, etc. I. Title.
GV1202.S87L37 2008
796.2—dc22

2006038826

On the cover: "Where we go one, we go all!" Battle drills are executed with scarce time to assess the situation or coordinate a response. The drill is executed in perfect order, as it has been rehearsed time and time again. Precision and violence are its momentum.

On the frontispiece: Swarming attacks are dispatched from either dispersed or massed locations. When massed, the swarming attack resembles bees coming out of a hive. When dispersed, the swarming attack resembles ants coming from multiple anthills onto a single target.

On the back cover, top: Crossing danger areas with the heart-shaped method makes maximum use of security and combat power. However, the heart-shaped method is time-consuming, making it impractical for small patrols who need to cross a small, linear danger area. **Middle:** The triangle method is the most common for light infantry patrol bases. This is because with a machine gun at each apex, an enemy approaching from any angle will be faced with at least one—and probably two—machine guns! **Bottom:** The raid has all of the same component teams as the ambush—security, support, and assault. The principle difference is the raid is conducted on stationary targets, whereas, the ambush is used on moving targets. Thus, raids require greater stealth.

About the author

Christopher E. Larsen has spent more than twenty years working with warriors from around the world. He holds the coveted title of Expert Infantry and has trained U.S. and foreign troops in Asia, the Mid East, and North America. Larsen currently serves as a military analyst–instructional systems designer for the U.S. Army's Command and General Staff College at Fort Leavenworth, Kansas.

Editor: Steve Gansen
Designer: Kou Lor

Printed in China

CONTENTS

ACKNOWLEDGMENTS

There are so many professional warriors who have helped me along my own path that I could not possibly list them all here. Still, I recognize your contributions to my progress as a warrior, and I've tried to capture the many lessons I learned along the way in these pages. I remember each of you. For your guidance, you have my sincere and profound thanks. This book would not be possible without your contributions.

Also, to my wonderful wife and partner, Hae-jung, for her tireless patience and support. I apologize for every chigger bite and ivy rash you picked up over the years while photographing One Shepherd in field environments. I realize it would have been infinitely easier on you if I had just picked up watching football. Sorry about that.

A very big thanks goes to John Gordon for his talented work on the schematics and to Billy Shackelford for his acute ability to keep me grounded, focused, and writing in active voice. Trust me—that's no small feat.

Finally, I have to thank Steve Gansen for championing my work, sight unseen. If he hadn't opened the doors for me, I'd still be fumbling through the streets with a "really great idea," and that simply doesn't buy a cup of coffee.

—*Christopher E. Larsen*

INTRODUCTION

The intention of this manual is to develop a tactical standard, as well as a tactical jargon, for the game of MilSim as it is played by paintballers and airsofters around the world. It is perpetually frustrating to have conversations on the gaming fields and discussion boards that include such expressions as, "You know—that leap froggish thing."

"Do you mean fire and maneuver? Or merely the potential to conduct fire and maneuver, in which case, you mean bound and overwatch?" Under fire, this conversation takes on a sort of surreal effect that's exasperating, if not nightmarish. Blech!

Now, I'm not suggesting we all become U.S. Navy SEAL Team qualified ninjas. That would require half a lifetime to learn this game. And, it is, after all, a game. We're supposed to have fun. On the other hand, who in their right mind would start a community baseball team with absolutely no intention to practice or even learn the sport?

Regrettably, that's just what has happened to MilSim over the last decade. Adventurous young men and women come together to form MilSim teams for paintball and airsoft—only to convince themselves that practice isn't necessary. Why? Because "tactics do not apply to MilSim."

And, there it is. Incredibly, this notion has spread throughout paintball and airsoft communities like wildfire! Even military veterans seem to have bought into this mantra and perpetuate it. Shocking! So, I will attempt to address some of the key arguments behind this misguided notion. As you'll see, this asinine belief is absolutely baseless:

ARGUMENT #1:

"The plastic BB and paintball have such a limited range that tactics are useless."

RESPONSE:

Wait a minute! This makes no sense at all. The Roman Legions, Napoleon's French Army, and the American Indians all had weapon systems with the same effective ranges as paintball and airsoft. They certainly used the tactics of their day with great success!

So, what does weapon range have to do with tactics? If your opponent significantly outranges your weapon, adapt your tactics and acquire longer-ranged weapons! Technological advantages are always temporary.

ARGUMENT #2:

"A bush or even blades of grass throw off the BB and paintball so severely that marksmanship and tactics are pointless."

RESPONSE:

A tree limb will bounce a hand grenade back at you if you don't throw it with care. So, we should abandon all tactics—or just grenades? Shouldn't we instead simply train troops to properly throw a hand grenade in such conditions? That seems more rational than abandoning all tactics.

Adjust tactics to the limitations of weapon systems. What weapon system is without limits?

ARGUMENT #3:

"Real weapons do not have a 300-round magazine capacity, but I can shoot a continuous burst of fire with my paintball/airsoft weapon. Therefore, tactics no longer apply to me."

RESPONSE:

History has shown time and time again that all technological advantages are temporary. The Confederate troops during the American Civil War did not abandon tactics merely because the Union troops had repeating rifles while the Confederates had muzzle-loading rifles. In fact, the Confederate tactics were quite good at mitigating the Union troops' advantage!

What's my point? It's two-fold. First, do not abandon tactics. Superior technology impacts tactics—*true*—but the force can adjust its tactics. Secondly, sooner or later, your opponent will get his hands on a weapon with a 300-round magazine capacity, too. Then it's a level playing field again, and you'll have to resort back to tactics.

ARGUMENT #4:

"No paintballer or airsofter is afraid of being hit. Without fear, tactics no longer apply."

RESPONSE:

At face value, that makes sense. However, history disproves this, too. Have you ever heard of the Chinese Boxer Rebellion, a Japanese Bonsai charge, or an Al Qaeda suicide bomber? In all of these examples, the enemies used suicide attacks with little regard for their own lives. That does not mean we stop using tactics just because the enemies are clearly willing to die for their causes!

ARGUMENT #5:

"I don't want to learn tactics. I just came here to shoot my friends and look cool."

RESPONSE:

Okay, I don't want to learn baseball either. I just want the bat beside my bed to club burglars on the noggin. But, then again, I don't go to the local baseball field, dressed and geared up, and complain that people are trying to force me to play the game.

If you're going to buy expensive equipment, dress up, drive out to the game field, and even take part in the game, you owe it to your buddies to at least understand how to play the game. It's called "MilSim." That means *military* simulation!

Tactics are common-sense solutions to battlefield problems. These solutions have been refined over the last 3,000 years. Once proven successful, they are accepted as "tactical doctrine." They're the cornerstone of battlefield successes—regardless of whether the battle uses real guns, paintballs, or slingshots!

If you practice the wrong way, you'll respond the wrong way in battle. If you practice correctly, you'll respond correctly in battle. That's the goal of tactics and tactical training—to get every member of the team responding perfectly.

Is perfection achievable? Yes. No. Maybe. Regardless, it is an honorable pursuit. More pertinently, this pursuit makes the difference between victory and failure, reward and frustration. This manual's intent is to provide you with a proven, workable tactical doctrine to get you and your team started on the right foot.

SECTION 1
BASIC INDIVIDUAL SKILLS

"No greater friend, nor worse foe." It is the individual infantryman who closes with the enemy to destroy or repel them in battle. It is the infantryman who pays for real estate in pain, sweat, and blood. He masters the art of the warrior and offers the hand of compassion. To achieve this, each troop must continue honing his or her field craft. The basis of all infantry field craft is the ability to shoot, move, communicate.

CHAPTER 1
WARRIOR SKILLS

CAMOUFLAGE

The first cardinal rule of battlefield survival: Don't become a casualty! Know how to disappear, or become a casualty. For all the complexity of modern targeting systems, it still holds true that if the enemy cannot find you, they will not shoot you. Mastering the art of camouflage allows you to disappear on the battlefield.

Why use this skill?

Camouflage is the ability to hide from enemy observation within the environment. This breaks down into two areas of concern—cover and concealment. *Cover* refers to all forms of protective obstacles from enemy fire, such as a tree, stone, wall, ditch, or hole in the ground. These obstacles provide some protection from flying projectiles. *Concealment* refers to the art of blending in with immediate surroundings. This is a form of protection from enemy observation, *not* protection from enemy fire!

Note: *Cover* is the act of hiding behind protective obstacles to avoid enemy fire. *Concealment* is the art of blending into the environment to avoid enemy observation.

It is best to apply camouflage in buddy teams because your buddy can always see flaws. Techniques for applying face grease typically fall into either "striping" or "splotching" patterns. Be sure to use colors that match the surrounding foliage.

Instructions

Camouflage includes the following considerations:

- Size—Similar-sized objects conceal more readily when together
- Shape—Rarely do perfect straight lines or circles appear in nature
- Shine—Typically caused by oils or smooth surfaces
- Shadow—Often give off patterns that are recognized even subconsciously
- Silhouette—An object is recognized when cast against a light background
- Texture—Not only the roughness of surfaces, but also the depth of view
- Color—The dominant color patterns in the immediate area

Camouflage Skin

The deep features of the face, such as the eyes, under the nose, curl of the lips, and jaw line, all lend to an immediately recognizable pattern of shadow that makes up the human face. Ever look at a grainy, poor-quality, black-and-white photograph? Even though you don't recognize the person in the picture, you are able to make out a human face. Well, those telltale features are actually just shadows thrown across the face of the person in the picture. Humans can recognize those shadow patterns even on inanimate objects, such as clouds or the moon!

These shadows must be filled in and distorted. To do this, use a light-colored cream or grease stick in a majority of the deep facial features, but don't just reverse the shadows, or you'll have the same pattern simply inverted! Use some dark colored creams or grease to "pull" the shadows out onto the forehead, cheeks, and neck. Break up the smooth prominent features—such as the nose, chin, and brow—by "cutting" them in half with the dark cream or grease. Remember to use colored grease and cream that match the dominant colors of your surroundings. For example, do not use a light gray if this is not a dominant color.

Lastly, repeat this color scheme on the backs of your hands if gloves are not worn. Hands typically move around much more than heads do. Since movement gives away concealment more than anything else, light-skinned hands moving around act like signaling flags! For crying out loud, darken those hands!

Camouflage Body and Gear

There are numerous and readily available camouflage patterns for uniforms. Truth be known, the troops often have little say-so about their uniforms because higher commands make these decisions. Often, the effort is toward uniformity—to all look the same.

Pretend for the moment you do not have a uniform. Fine. You must dress in colors that match your environment or, at least, the dominant single color. If in a jungle, the easy choice is green. That would be a tan color if in a desert, white if in snow tundra, and so on. The good news is that load-bearing

The naturally occurring shadows of the human face can be recognized even on non-human objects. The "man in the moon" is a bit cartoonish, but his open-mouthed face is evident from the large shadows of his eyes looking up and left.

equipment (LBE) breaks up solid-colored clothing by casting shadows. To break up the solid colors of limbs, simply wrap friction tape around arms and legs. This not only breaks up the color scheme, but it also secures baggy clothing from flapping and getting caught on things. Careful not to wrap the tape so tightly that fingers turn blue and feet shrink.

As mentioned earlier, work gloves are great for camouflaging hands. Even in hot climates, wear gloves with the fingers cut out. Gloves have the added benefit of protecting against scratches, cuts, and bug bites.

Hair is another easily recognized human feature in nature, so troops cover their heads with the appropriate color scheme. Use a hat, bandana, or helmet, or suffer the consequences!

Also, cover gear. LBE, bandoleers, canteens, and rucksack all need to hide as well. Tape all metal rings, snaps, and closures. This will make them quiet, as well as reduce the shine. There are a great many forms of plastic vegetation in craft shops, or tear off 30 cm x 30 cm pieces of artillery netting or strips of colored burlap. In lieu of these fantastic camouflage materials, use the real thing—vegetation from the surroundings. The down side of real vegetation is that it is difficult to fasten to gear, and even then, it wilts and dies quickly, but you can periodically replace it. There's plenty of it!

One of the key aims of camouflage is to break up naturally occurring shadows. Use dark colors on prominent features, such as the brow, nose, and chin. Then use light colors in the recessed areas and pull the colors into an unnatural pattern.

The art of camouflage does not end with face grease. Weapon, uniform, and equipment all must blend into the surroundings, too. In a modern world of high-tech targeting systems, camouflage is more critical now than ever! Be creative.

The importance of camouflage is often overlooked with the advent of more sophisticated targeting systems, but that makes camouflage all the more necessary. Creativity should be encouraged, but as in all things, use moderation. If camouflage attracts attention, it's too much camouflage!

Hand and Arm Signals
Most of the communication on the battlefield is conducted by waving hands above heads in a seemingly spastic series of gestures.

Signal with either hand while holding a weapon in the other hand. Also, with the exception of the rally point signal, all hand and arm signals are passed back to the next member of the patrol immediately! This is true even if the next troop has already seen the signal. Why? Because formations take many shapes, and it's never certain who in the formation might be turning about, facing out, or looking down. All members of the patrol repeating the hand and arm signal greatly increases the chance everyone sees and understands it.

Why Use This Skill?

Signals are used when noise discipline must be maintained. Hand and arm signals are also used over long distances, with most signals easily recognized as far as a quarter mile (four hundred meters) away. Finally, over the chaotic roar of battle, hand and arm signals can still be understood.

The mistake many leaders make is believing that, during the firefight, hand and arm signals are still the preferred method of communication. Not true. After all, the enemy knows where the patrol is because the two forces are shooting back and forth at each other. The best communication at this point is to use voice *augmented* with signals. Command troops quickly and assertively. Do not distract troops with stylish delivery of hand and arm signals! They need to watch their sectors of fire!

Instructions

Twenty standard hand and arm signals follow. Patrols will come up with other signals carrying unique meanings to teammates.

"I Am Ready"

Meaning the troop is ready to receive a command. This is often called the "yoo-hoo" wave, and it is used most often to gain the attention of another unit leader.

"I Do Not Understand"

This signal means the troop does not understand the last message or cannot comply with the last command. It is also referred to as the "wave off."

Formally, the "I Do Not Understand" signal is given by shielding your entire face with both hands, palms facing out. Of course, this is ridiculous because you cannot hold your weapon in your hand since, like several other hand and arm signals, it requires the use of both hands! A common variation of this signal is to use only one hand, palm facing out, and wave it left and right to the side of your midsection, thus, known as the "wave off."

"Move Out"

This means all members of the patrol should begin movement forward.

The "I Am Ready" signal is given by waving an open-palm hand as if saying "hello" across the parking lot.

The "Move Out" signal is given by raising an arm straight up into the air and letting it fall forward. Often, the arm is only raised up from the elbow and dropped forward. This is due largely to the weight of the LBE and rucksack pinching and fatiguing the shoulders. The signal looks about the same in either case.

"Stop"

Means the patrol will halt, but you may continue to move to protective cover. *Do not* confuse this with the hand signal "freeze!" With the "stop" signal, there is no known threat to the patrol.

Give the "Stop" signal by simply pushing a flattened palm toward the intended receiver, as if you were politely refusing a caramel-covered snail. If you enjoy the taste of caramel-covered snails . . . well . . . there is something very wrong with you.

"Freeze!"

Meaning, *don't move!* Don't step forward, speak, or even turn your head to look for cover. This signal indicates danger is very close, such as an enemy patrol passing by, or land mines. Do not over-use this signal. You should not use this signal when you simply want the patrol to stop.

The "Freeze!" signal is given by making a quick fist, palm outward. Do not wave the fist about. Simply hold your hand level, and continue to make it until the intended receiver understands.

"Get Down/Lower"

This signal means lower your profile closer to the ground so you cannot be seen.

Give the "Get Lower" signal by pushing a flattened palm toward the ground, which is fairly basic stuff.

"Get Up/Higher"

Meaning you should raise your profile and be prepared to move.

Give the "Get Up" signal by pushing a flattened palm toward the sky.

"Increase Intervals"

Meaning there needs to be greater space between individuals in the formation or between formations. This signal is often given when a patrol is passing from heavy vegetation to lighter vegetation or onto a road.

Formally, the "Increase Interval" signal is given by placing two hands with palms facing outward, then pushing them apart to increase the space between the hands. An acceptable variation of this signal, due to carrying a weapon, is simply to place one hand against the side of the rifle and pull them apart in the same manner.

"Decrease Intervals"

This means that the space between troops needs to tighten up. This signal is often given as a patrol enters heavier vegetation, just before passing an obstacle, or before overwhelming an enemy position.

The "Decrease Interval" signal is formally given by pushing two flattened palms together over your head. An acceptable variation is to push one flattened palm to the side of your rifle.

"Column File"

This signal means the patrol will form a single-line formation in a follow-the-leader fashion. This is also called the "Ranger file" or "column of ducks."

The "Column File" signal is given by raising an arm straight up in the air, then making a backward circle as if you were doing the backstroke with one arm. You'll feel silly at first, but everyone gets this one. It's the exact *opposite* rotation of the signal "move out."

"Wedge"

Meaning the patrol should assume the inverted "V" formation within their fireteams and prepare to attack.

Give the "Wedge" signal by raising straightened arms up slightly from your hips so your arms form the shape of an upside-down "V." This can be done with rifle in hand.

"On Line"

Meaning the entire element should come into a line to my immediate left and right. Often given just prior to overwhelming an enemy position or when making a hasty defensive line.

"Patch to the Road"

Meaning the patrol will cross a linear danger area using the "patch-to-the-road" method, and all troops in the patrol should *close up the intervals* between members shoulder-to-shoulder.

Give the "On Line" signal by raising straightened arms up level with your shoulders like you are walking a suspended tightrope. This can also be done with rifle in hand.

The "Patch-to-the-Road" signal is given by patting the unit patch twice, rapidly. The patch is located on your upper *left* arm. Be certain that the troop behind you sees this signal. In short, turn your left shoulder toward the intended receiver of this signal.

"Danger Area"

Meaning a dangerous area is immediately in front of the point man—typically indicating some type of open or linear clearing.

Give the "Danger Area" signal by moving a flattened hand back and forth across the neck in a cutting fashion. Again, with all the weight of gear, this requires much less effort than earlier versions of this signal.

"Patrol Leader"

Meaning the designated patrol leader should move up the formation.

Give the "Patrol Leader" signal by patting your *forehead* two times softly, like several quick salutes from the center of your forehead. Variations of this include tapping your mid-chest several times for the squad or element leader or your groin several times for a fireteam leader.

"Security Team"

Meaning the designated security team should move up the formation.

The "Security Team" signal is given by pointing your index and middle fingers just under your eyes. Be careful not to poke yourself in the eyes. It is very painful, and there is no need to get that close to your eyes. We all get the meaning.

"Rally Point"

This is the location (big tree, big stone, fence, meadow) where the patrol will rally if necessary in the near future. It is normally given after every major terrain feature, or 300 meters.

Give the "Rally Point" signal by making a short circle directly above your head, then drop your arm dramatically and point to the exact location of the designated rally position.

"Rally on Me"

Meaning the entire patrol must come to my position and form a tight circular security.

Give the "Rally on Me" signal by raising a straightened arm directly above your head and, with fingers stiffened, make short circles as if you were trying to draw a hole in the sky.

Note: This is one of those few hand and arm signals that will *not* pass back down the formation immediately. Only as each troop passes the rally point will they pass this signal back. They *must* get a confirming nod of the head from the receiver to be certain the message will be passed along in turn.

"Prepare for Action!"

This signal means to expect enemy contact in this given direction very soon—often when suspicious voices or troop movement is heard.

Give the "Prepare for Action" signal by quickly punching a fist several times in the direction you believe the enemy is coming.

Note: This is *not* an order to begin firing! The source of the noise or movement has not been confirmed yet. If it had been, the "Enemy in Sight" signal would have been given.

"Enemy in Sight"

Meaning visual contact with the enemy. This signal is *only* for confirmed visual contact with the enemy.

The "Enemy in Sight" signal is given by making a fist with the thumb pointed down and the index finger pointed forward. The hand signal is first shown to members of the patrol and then thrust in the direction of the enemy. An acceptable variation is to raise your rifle above your head—magazine pointed skyward—and point the muzzle toward the enemy. Of course, this is an idiotic maneuver and should only be done when passing this information over a very large distance.

The habit of repeating signals has a double benefit. First, it tells the individual sending the message that his message was understood. Second, if the intended recipient of the message was looking away and did not receive the signal, every member in the patrol repeating it significantly increases the probability that the intended recipient *will* see another patrol member repeating the message.

Each member of the patrol should periodically look backward or forward. As a general rule of thumb, turn to look behind you about every sixth step of the left foot. This makes sure you'll receive the hand and arm signals being passed up from the rear. It is critical that everyone be informed.

INDIVIDUAL MOVEMENT TECHNIQUES

Troops must move, advancing upon or withdrawing from the enemy. This chapter looks at individual movement techniques (IMTs).

Use IMTs when under enemy fire or when attempting to avoid enemy detection through stealth. Stealth is achieved partially through "noise discipline," meaning the use of hand and arm signals, and partially through "light discipline," which includes camouflage. Since movement is easiest for the human eye to detect, the proper choice of IMT is important for stealth.

Why Use This Skill?

IMTs are common-sense methods of moving from one covered position to the next. The goal of IMT is to minimize exposure to the enemy's view and/or hearing so they are unlikely to shoot in the patrol's direction. This is true even when already engaged in a firefight. A degree of stealth minimizes the amount of enemy fire directed toward the patrol.

Instructions

After watching a squad use these techniques to cross terrain, the untrained eye may mistakenly conclude that the squad adheres to IMTs in the sloppiest forms. That's one view. Another view is that experienced troops move quickly from one technique to another, so their movement seems to be an improvised collection of these techniques. As sloppy as this often looks, IMTs have a practical application and must suit the needs of the troop—not the other way around.

The Low Crawl

This technique is used when receiving incoming grazing fire at knee level. The low crawl is very slow and exhausting. Furthermore, because of the dragging nature of the low crawl, it is rarely ever used for stealth. In forested or grassy areas, the noise of the dragging would likely give away your position. However, this technique does flatten soldiers' bodies and allows them to hug the contour of the ground. That's effective for avoiding intense, low-level fire!

The low crawl requires lying prone on the belly with the side of the head pressed firmly against the ground. Look only for the next covered position. Cradle the weapon so the muzzle will not become obstructed with dirt and mud. Then, move

Use the low crawl IMT when incoming fire is as low as knee-high. The troops cannot even raise their head or limbs for fear of being shot! They must move by grabbing earth to push and pull themselves along. It is very slow and exhausting.

forward by pushing and pulling earth, grass, and roots. Again, this is a very slow and exhausting form of IMT.

The low crawl is absolutely the filthiest of all the IMTs because your body must maintain contact with the ground. Do *not* raise your head to see what is going on around you, nor should you raise your limbs to help push off. If it is raining, be prepared to have mud caked into every imaginable crevice.

The High Crawl
Use this technique when receiving incoming grazing fire at hip level. The high crawl is as exhausting as the low crawl,

though it does allow a somewhat faster pace. Again, due to the noisy, dragging nature of this crawl, it would not be used for stealth in most environments.

The high crawl also requires lying prone on the belly, however, this technique allows you to keep your head upright, giving you greater situational awareness and navigation, and it's just a little cleaner.

Using this technique, determine the next covered position. Place your weapon on safe and cradle it to protect it from dirt and debris. Then, move forward by pushing and pulling with knees and elbows.

Use the high crawl IMT when incoming fire is at waist level. The troops can safely lift their heads and limbs to propel themselves forward, but this movement is still very slow and exhausting. Both the low crawl and high crawl require friendly cover fire.

Also known as the "baby crawl" or "spider crawl," use the modified crawl IMT when incoming fire is chest-high or higher. The modified crawl is much faster and less exhausting than the other two crawls. It's also less noisy and, therefore, stealthier.

The Modified Crawl

This technique is used when receiving incoming fire above grazing level—about chest-high. The modified crawl allows you to be up on your hands and knees to move. When moving slowly, this crawl offers excellent stealth! When used quickly, the modified crawl covers terrain much faster than the other two crawls. That is very important because speed is a form of security: troops are exposed to enemy detection and fire for a shorter span of time moving from cover to cover.

Like the other two techniques, the modified crawl requires you to visually identify the next covered position. Come up on hands and knees, cradle the weapon in one arm, and use the other arm and legs to crawl forward. Obviously, with head up, you can easily monitor the battlefield and communicate with other team members.

The modified crawl is much less messy and less exhausting than the other two techniques.

The Rush

This technique is used when receiving sporadic incoming fire. More specifically, use the rush when absolutely certain the enemy is not shooting at you! The rush uses speed as its primary source of security, and indeed, the rush is very fast. As a general rule, troops are allowed only three seconds of exposure!

Three seconds is just enough time to say, "I'm up. They see me. I'm down." Any longer than that, and the enemy machine gunner will send something unpleasant. So, look

Use the rush IMT when incoming fire is sporadic—when you're certain the enemy is not aiming at you! Like all IMT, an overwatch element must cover this IMT. In this case, the buddy provides cover.

for the next covered position, place your weapon on safe, hop up to your feet, and sprint forward—no longer than three seconds. Once on the ground, roll left or right so the enemy gunners don't know where you will come up next. Remember, they just saw exactly where you went down. They'll be watching for you to come up again from that same spot.

The term "bound" can mean to run or walk, but the term "rush" implies running. Because you crash to the ground behind your next covered position, the rush is not very useful when stealth is required. When 200 pounds of body weight and combat load goes running across the ground, boots thump incredibly loud! The weapon smacks into rock and earth, canteens bump against body armor and magazines, and the radio whacks into the side of your helmet.

In movies, the bad guys don't hear the ninjas jumping from tree to tree and falling to earth. That's called "suspension of disbelief." It works in Hollywood. It doesn't work in real life. The bottom line is that running through the forest is not a very stealthy thing to do. If planned well, the troops only have to run when the shooting starts.

Individuals Bound by Buddy Team

On a battlefield, two are better than one. Two-man teams working together are much more efficient at moving forward, regardless of which technique is chosen.

The drill of bounding by buddy team uses these same four IMTs. One troop provides suppressive fire—or at least overwatch with the intention of suppressing any potential enemy—while the other troop moves forward. In this manner, the enemy's view of the exposed troop is further impaired.

This technique requires some coordination between buddy team members. When under fire, coordination is achieved by yelling because buddy teams are generally just a few meters from each other. In situations requiring stealth, communication may be achieved with whispers or hand and arm signals.

- The forward troop takes a position that allows a view of potential threats.
- The forward troop calls "Set" to signal he is in position.
- The trailing troop calls "Cover me" to signal he is beginning movement.
- The trailing troop selects the next position, the IMT, and moves out.
- The lead troop fires for suppression when necessary.
- Once the trailing troop gets to the next covered position, he readies his weapon and calls "Set."

This cycle continues until the two-man buddy team reaches their objective. On large battlefields, rests and water

One buddy team uses an IMT while the other buddy team provides overwatch and/or cover fire. IMT used with covering fire are the basic building blocks of any offensive mission. Simply build from there—such as fireteams or squads covering each other.

breaks will be factored in. Be sure to mix up the routine so it does not become predictable to enemy gunners. For example, the forward troop will bound two or more times before calling the trail troop forward.

Buddy Teams Bound by Fireteam

Now, if two troops are more effective than one in maneuvering forward, then buddy teams moving in coordinated bounds across a battlefield would be very impressive! After all, that's how building blocks work. Start with the individual, then in pairs, then in fireteams, then squads, and platoons, and so on. Just remember to keep it simple, and keep everyone focused on the same goal.

When a fireteam moves across an objective under fire, it will deploy its two-man buddy teams in much the same way as an individual troop. One buddy team acts together, shoulder-to-shoulder, to set a base of fire and suppress the enemy position. The buddy team moves forward together, using the appropriate IMT and the most concealed route available. Once the bounding buddy team reaches its intended position, that buddy team assumes the task of offering a base of fire. The forward buddy team then calls back to the other, and the process repeats.

This leapfrog procession continues until the squad has successfully crossed and secured the far side of the objective, or until the squad is so near to the enemy fighting positions that a mad charge into the enemy line is coordinated and ordered by the fireteam leader.

Getting It Right

IMTs and moving troops across the battlefield appear to be fairly intuitive, and they are. However, simple procedures often involve subtle complexities that may not be immediately apparent. This is definitely true when moving troops under fire. There are three tendencies troops fall into while conducting this task, and all three of these tendencies present significant danger. They are:

- Muzzle creep
- Glancing back
- Funneling

Muzzle creep means that as the troops IMT forward, they become slipshod as to where their weapons are pointing. The intensity of combat on the objective with outgoing and incoming fire requires a great deal of discipline in muzzle control. The danger here is fratricide. Therefore, it is the individual's responsibility to be certain that his weapon is *always* pointing in the suspected direction of the enemy!

Glancing back refers to the habit of troops looking back over their shoulder when they should be looking forward or placing suppressive fire forward. It is understandable that troops need to glance back to communicate. However, the bounding element is relying solely on the overwatch element to suppress the enemy or potential threat. This cannot be done effectively if the troops on the overwatch are looking back over their shoulders to "see what's taking the bounding team so long." It is the team leader's responsibility to communicate with other elements. Everyone else must face forward. This habit must be broken by a combined effort of the individual and fireteam leader to ensure effective, suppressive fire is placed on the objective.

Funneling is the phenomenon of troops massing together in the middle of the objective. Troops aren't stupid. They can see who the bad guys are and have a clear understanding of the threat to themselves and their buddies. When crossing an objective, troops often move in a direct line toward the threat. This is particularly true if a threat has just been eliminated. The troops do this to be certain the threat has been eliminated! They may also be attempting to communicate with other team members in order to identify other threats and such.

Bunching together on the objective presents some very real dangers to the team. When an assault funnels on the objective, they become an easy target for the enemy. What's more, the areas just to the left, right, and rear of the objective are not secured. The assault becomes vulnerable to counterassaults.

It is the fireteam leader's responsibility to keep the team moving across the objective and to seize the far side. Remember, each troop should be assigned a position in the online formation as a matter of SOP. That way, he always knows who will be on his right and who will be on his left. This helps to form the sweep across the objective and to keep troops from funneling toward the threat.

IMTs are methods of moving from one covered position to the next that minimize exposure to enemy fire or detection. The four techniques include the low crawl for fire at knee level, the high crawl for fire at hip level, the modified crawl for fire at chest level, and the rush for sporadic incoming fire.

IMTs are the building blocks for team movement. Individuals move as part of a buddy team. Buddy teams move as part of a fireteam. Fireteams move as part of a squad, and so on.

Other than for demonstrative purposes or practice, IMTs should *not* be utilized with strict regard to form. IMTs are used to suit specific needs while maneuvering across hostile ground. Contrary to the military practice of using these techniques as a form of punitive exercise, exhausting troops is not the goal. Instead, select the safest, least exhausting method to move toward or away from enemy fire.

FIGHTING POSITIONS

Not to be a killjoy, but fighting positions do not deal with the proper stances of hand-to-hand combat. There will be nothing as gung-ho as disarming a knife-wielding opponent in this chapter. Instead, this chapter explores . . . uh, well, dirt.

While fighting positions might appear to be a somewhat mundane subject, this topic is far more applicable to the modern battlefield than all of that macho hand-to-hand nonsense. Fighting positions offer a great deal of protection from projectiles constantly flying about the battlefield. In a hole or behind a barrier, the body is almost entirely lower than the surface of the ground. That's good because the enemy's weapons will not fire through earth, rock, and wood.

Why Use This Skill?

Fighting positions offer cover and concealment from enemy fire and observation. From the relative security of fighting positions, the advancing enemy is faced with the near- impossible task of shooting troops in the head.

Of course, realizing the enemy's task is to shoot you in the head would give any sane person reason to pause. At least to some degree, it will be necessary to expose heads and arms in order to return fire against an enemy. Just remember, the advancing enemy has to expose his entire body, while you only expose a small portion of yours. Running around exposed to enemy view and fire is the worst possible place to be on a battlefield. On the other hand, hunkered down in a hole and shooting at the unfortunate souls running amuck is the best possible place. That is why soldiers habitually dig holes.

Instructions

What follows are several examples of common, two-man fighting positions, discussion of when each position should be used, and the physical dimensions of each type.

Barricades

This is the simplest fighting position and only offers protection to the immediate front. The barricade is most commonly formed with sandbags but may be improvised with stones or logs of at least eight inches (20 cm) thick. Then, reinforce it with earth or sand. The barricade must be a minimum of 20 inches (50 cm) thick at the top—no less than two sandbags.

Camouflage the barricade so it is not immediately noticeable from 35 meters forward of the position. Place 6- to 8-inch cuts of grass sod over the front, top, and sides. If not in a grassy environment, use the appropriate amount of leaves, sticks, snow, or sand. Be certain to gather this camouflage material from BEHIND your position!

Hasty Fighting Positions

This fighting position is also called "the shell scrape" by commonwealth troops. The hasty fighting position is for temporary use only. It is intended to lower the body of a troop lying prone to just below the surface of the earth. The troop's body should not be observable from 35 meters in front of the position.

The hasty fighting position is located with a sizable obstacle to the front, such as a tree, mound of earth, or boulder. The dimensions of the hasty position should be roughly two and-a-half feet wide (75 cm), one foot (30 cm) deep, and as long as the length of that particular troop.

These fighting positions have been around since the days of the Roman Legionnaires and can still be found on Rome's furthest frontiers. The barricade offers immediate cover and concealment from frontal fire—as long as it is constructed durably!

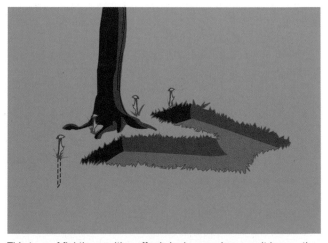

This type of fighting position affords body cover because it lowers the entire profile just below the surface of the earth. Incredibly, it takes very little earth to protect us from incoming fire at shallow angles!

The hasty position forms a "V" shape when viewed from above, with both men's feet meeting. This allows them to quietly kick each other to alert status.

Light Fighting Positions

Because tanks and armored vehicles rarely support light infantry troops, they often dig fighting positions without parapets. This position lowers the silhouette of the fighting position to the level of the ground's surface and makes for an almost impossible target. It also makes the position nearly impervious to rocket attack.

Rockets are very effective against fighting positions. However, rockets need a surface to slam into to detonate. This position offers no protruding obstacles, so rockets fly right overhead unless attack helicopters fire them from a steep angle. In that case, the rocket would have to actually strike the overhead cover or land directly in the hole. That wouldn't be very pleasant, but whatcha gonna do?

1. Locate the fighting position so it's approximately level to, or higher than, the enemy's expected approach.
2. The position's dimensions are feet (1 meter) wide, 10 feet long (3 meters), and armpit-deep to each particular troop. This means one end of the position may be deeper than the other due to differences in each troop's height.
3. As the fighting position is dug, all earth is carried behind the defensive line and dispersed. This is done so the enemy cannot see fresh dirt from the front.
4. To the middle front and middle back of the position, dig a platform three feet (1 meter) wide and 20 inches (50 cm) deep. This platform will support the overhead cover.

5. Lay in the overhead cover at least 18 inches thick, using a combination of fresh-cut logs, a rain sheet, and sandbags. Use 6 inches of grass sod or appropriate materials to camouflage the overhead cover. This will compress down quickly.

When finished, the position should look like two square holes in the earth when viewed from above. Camouflage the fighting position so it blends with the natural environment when viewed from 35 meters in front. Hammer aiming stakes into the ground so anyone occupying the fighting position will understand the left and right limit of fire—even at night.

Advanced Fighting Positions

The advanced fighting position has the exact same dimensions as the light fighting position. The key difference is overhead cover. The advanced fighting position builds up parapets to the front, sides, and back, which raise the elevation of the overhead cover. The parapets lend added protection from small arms fire and shrapnel during artillery barrages. Additionally, the parapets protect the troops in the fighting position when tanks, armored vehicles, and artillery guns are firing support. That saves having limbs ripped off by a muzzle blast from a friendly main gun!

The obvious disadvantage of the advanced fighting position is that it is more vulnerable to rocket attack, but remember tanks and armored vehicles have sophisticated targeting systems and standoff weaponry. That's why mechanized infantry are far more likely to use the advanced fighting position—because they often defend with all of these resources integrated into their units.

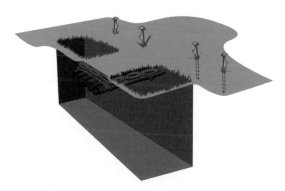

Full two-man fighting positions can be constructed with parapets or without. Here is a fighting position without parapets—protection to the side and rear for troops firing from the position. This position is very difficult to target!

Throughout time, the barricade has been one of the most common hasty fighting positions because it offers cover for the most vital angle—the front! Carefully camouflage the positions so they cannot be seen from 35 meters forward.

Fighting positions offer cover and concealment from enemy fire and observation. They are not placed randomly but are established in coordination with a defensive line or defensive perimeter. Select the appropriate fighting position depending on the needs of the mission and time available.

Digging a fighting position—particularly one with overhead cover—takes considerable time. It is hard and noisy work. For this reason, one troop of each buddy team should ensure forward security while the other troop works. Obviously, these shifts should be rotated to conserve energy.

TACTICAL COMMUNICATIONS

Shoot, move, and communicate. These are the basic combat skills. There are numerous communicative systems. These include visual, auditory, oral, and electronic systems. The earlier section on hand and arm signals is one example of visual communication, but visual communication also includes the use of signal flags, lights, pyrotechnic flares, and smoke. Auditory communication systems include whistles, sirens, gongs, or bells. Oral communications involve the use of vocal commands and messengers, often referred to as "runners."

Each system has its advantages and disadvantages. For example, use of runners may not be the quickest or most reliable communication, yet it does represent the most secure form of communication. If you want to send a message you absolutely cannot afford the enemy to intercept, a runner is the wisest choice. Selection of communication method depends greatly on the needs of the mission. At least one other system should back up all communication systems in case the primary system fails.

Why Use This Skill?
This section will explore the use of transmitting devices. Electronic transmitting devices fall into two basic categories— **field telephones**, which transmit by wire, and **radios**, which transmit broadcasts.

Arguably, computer-based transmissions should be included in this chapter. However, operations using computer-based communication currently take place at higher echelons of command and, therefore, aren't as applicable to small-unit tactics. With the advent of new technologies, this notion is quickly changing!

Instructions
Field Phone Operations
Field phones use wire. In this way, phones are more secure than radios because they do not transmit radio waves, which

Broadcast communication is vulnerable to interception. Even the venerable landline wire can be tapped and monitored. For all the technological advances in science, the runner is still the most secure form of communication, though certainly not the fastest. However, field phones over the landline come in a close second.

are easy to intercept. As a general rule, if wire is secure, the transmission is secure. Of course, the team will have to physically lay the wire from one position to the next, and the length of that wire limits mobility. These are the obvious disadvantages of a field telephone. Less obvious is that weather, vehicles, and the enemy can damage the wire. There must be considerable care when laying and securing wire.

Laying and Securing Wire: The wire should be laid in reverse order, starting at the end point and running to the beginning point. This allows the operator at the beginning point the option of either rolling up the wire at the end of its use or cutting the wire to make a quick withdraw while preserving the remainder of the wire on the spool.

The wire is tied to a ground stake at its end point, leaving enough loose running wire to maneuver the phone within the fighting position. Then, the wire spool is unrolled, passing through each user station until reaching the beginning point. Be certain there is plenty of slack in the wire, which allows ease of future maintenance. The wire must be tied to a ground stake at the beginning point with the remainder of the spool.

One technique for laying wire requires that the wire be secured to a stake or tree every so many meters. This is advisable for long-term static positions but less feasible for a position that requires the wire to be gathered quickly.

Satellite, computer, radio, field phone, pyrotechnics, and runners—there are many forms of communication, and it is a safe bet that the chaos of battle will be enough to strain any single system to the point of failure. It's best to back each system up with at least two others.

runs off two D-cell batteries and a hand crank. Many NATO variations of this field phone are available commercially.

Perhaps the most versatile field phone is the TA-1. It is much lighter, at only 3.5 pounds (1.6 kg), has a range of up to sixteen kilometers, and uses no batteries. It includes an indigenous hand-squeezed generator that powers all transmissions. The ringer can be adjusted in sound all the way down to the silent mode, which activates a luminous dial alert for incoming calls. This field phone is available commercially.

Radio Operations

Two-way radios are the most convenient means of communication and are indispensable on combat patrols! No other system of communication matches their immediacy, mobility, and range. The down side is that the enemy easily monitors radios.

A great deal of time and money has been spent on trying to maximize radio to counter monitoring activities, but the most effective counter to monitoring is the creation of code. The U.S. Army formally refers to its codebook as Signal Operating Instructions (SOI). The U.S. Marine Corps calls its codebook the Communications-Electronic Operating Instructions (CEOI). Though the SOI and CEOI are essentially identical terms, we will use the easier SOI.

The SOI collects all pertinent codes in one written work. This work includes the codes to encrypt and decrypt messages and numbers, establish frequencies, recognize other friendly units using the radio, challenge unrecognized users, and establish passwords to recognize these friendly units when coming face-to-face with them.

Once the wire is laid and secured, the beginning station, end station, and stations in between can separate and splice the wire to attach their field phones. This system allows multiple user stations. It is called a "hot loop." When a station generates a call to another station, all the stations in the hot loop receive that call alert and can take part in the communication.

Since field phones are so much more secure than radios, there are no hard-and-fast rules for procedural language. Each station will transmit their messages in the shortest, most direct manner, though common radio procedures tend to be used.

Phone Variations: Because they are more secure than radio devices, field phones are an excellent choice for defensive positions. Many types of field phones are commercially available through military surplus, and most function very well with ranges over ten kilometers. Though a bit heavy, the U.S.–manufactured TA-312 is an excellent field phone that

Even the most impressive military can fail if it cannot coordinate its efforts. Tactical communications enable the patrol to do just that—coordinate. Modern technologies use satellite systems to communicate literally around the world.

SOI Creation and Use: Creating your own SOI is surprisingly simple. Print and copy all necessary information on note cards. Laminate these cards against the environment. Distribute the SOI to each radio operator. The RTO fastens the SOI to an arm, around the neck with a cord, or inside the top of headgear.

The SOI contains critical information that must never fall into the hands of the enemy. If the SOI is compromised, issue a new SOI as soon as possible! Never use an SOI longer than twenty-four hours, and preferably no more than twelve hours. Then, collect the SOI, and issue a new one to the RTO.

Below is an example of a homemade company-level SOI. Printed front and back on a single piece of paper, it fits nicely in a hat or taped to the inside of the forearm:

Call signs: Although you may adjust the call sign portion of the SOI to fit your own needs, this pattern is fairly comprehensive for a company-sized unit. At first glance, you will recognize only nine call signs, but in fact, there are thirty-one call signs on this card for an entire company of 100-150 troops. That breaks down into ten call signs for the three platoons, three call signs for each squad, and one call sign for each fireteam.

One of the most difficult things to remember is that the numbers and letters of these call signs are selected at random. That means the numbers and letters don't refer to a specific order or meaning. The highest-ranking troop does not start at "one" or "A." If the signs have meaning, the enemy will quickly compromise the code. So, each SOI randomly alters everyone's call sign.

SIGNAL OPERATING INSTRUCTION CARD

(Front)

CALL SIGN		SITREP	
Company Commander	FOX98	Moving	DOG
1st Platoon Leader	ZULU 25	Halted	COW
1st Squad Leader	40	In	ORPSHEEP
Alpha Team Leader	40MIKE	At	OBJCAT
Bravo Team Leader	40TANGO	Enemy Spotted	GOAT
2nd Squad Leader	72	Compromised	HAMSTER
3rd Squad Leader	22	Have Casualties	PIG
2ND Platoon Leader	BRAVO 25	Mission Complete	HORSE
3rd Platoon Leader	ROMEO 25		

EXHAUSTION			
1 2 3 4 5 6 7 8 9 0		Challenge: RED	Password: SMILE
		Running Password: BUDWEISER	
AUTHENTICATION TABLE		**PASSWORDS**	

(Back)

ORDERS		RESOURCES	
Move	EAGLE	Ammunition	ELEPHANT
Halt	HOUND	Batteries	DEER
Attack	QUAIL	Water	BEAR
Withdraw	PIDGEON	Food	SNAKE
Continue Mission	GRIZZLY	Reinforcements	RABBIT
Rendezvous	WEASEL	More Time	WOLF
At/To "—-"	SNAPPER	I Request "—-"	FROG
Until/NLT "—-"	HAWK		
Yes (Granted)	TURTLE	What's Our SitRep?	BADGER
No (Denied)	CHICKEN	What's Our Location?	EEL
ANSWERS		**QUESTIONS**	

Here is how it breaks down. On this card, the *company commander's* call sign is F98 or "Fox Nine-Eight." Any RTO working for the commander uses this call sign. If another calling station wanted to speak directly to the commander, ask for the "Fox nine-eight Actual." The term "Actual" means the actual person for whom this call sign was designated.

Similarly, a *platoon leader's* call sign will include a letter followed by two numbers. The first letter designates their platoon. The following two numbers are his personal identification. So, the 1st Platoon Leader's call sign is the "Z" designator for 1st Platoon and "25" for the personal identification—Zulu Two-Five. The 2nd Platoon Leader's call sign is the "B" designator for that platoon, followed by "25"—Bravo Two-Five. And 3rd Platoon Leader is Romeo Two-Five. *Squad leaders* use the same letter designator their platoon leader uses, plus a personal identification. For example, the 1st squad leader of 1st platoon would use the "Z" and personal ID number of "40," so Zulu Four-Zero Zulu Seven-Two would be the 2nd squad leader of 1st platoon, and Zulu Two-Two would indicate the 3rd squad leader—all in 1st platoon. Then 2nd Platoon follows suit—Bravo Four-Zero is the first squad leader of 2nd Platoon, Romeo Four-Zero is the first squad leader of 3rd Platoon, and so on.

Fireteam leaders use the same platoon designated number *and* their squad leader's number but have a letter designator added to the end of the call sign. So, the alpha fireteam leader of 3rd Platoon would use the "R," and since he was from 3rd Squad he would use the number "22." Finally, the personal identification letter "M" would be attached to his call sign, so Romeo Two-Two Mike. The bravo fireteam leader of this same squad and same platoon is Romeo Two-Two Tango.

Remember, these numbers and letters are selected at random. They don't have any real meaning of their own. Think of it like a number on a football jersey. Does the number "01" indicate this player is the quarterback of the team? No. So, even though it makes logical sense, Alpha One-One Alpha is *not* A Company, 1st Platoon, 1st Squad, A Fireteam. If it were, the enemy would compromise the code quickly!

Encryption of messages: This is a lot of fun, and the system is pretty straightforward. The code words—also called brevity codes—are random and relate in some fashion. This SOI used animals but could have just as easily used cars, major European cities, body parts, brand names of wristwatches, anything! The important thing is not to assign meaning. For example, don't use "Tiger" for the attack order and "Chicken" for withdraw. These words have too much connotative meaning, so try to be random.

For example, a commander or platoon leader may want to ask a patrol for their situation report (SITREP). The commander would simply identify himself using the call sign, and after making contact send the question:

Commander: "Romeo Two-Five, this is Fox Nine-Eight, over."

Patrol: "This is Romeo Two-Five, over."

Commander: "Romeo Two-Five, interrogative. I send Badger, over."

Patrol: "Roger, Fox Nine-Eight, I copy Badger. Wait one, over. This is Romeo Two-Five, I send Sheep, over."

Commander: "Roger, Romeo Two-Five, I copy Sheep, out."

As complicated as this sounds, it's actually quite simple. The commander called up the patrol and identified himself. Once the patrol responded, the commander said, "I have a question. What's your SITREP?" The patrol responded, "Yeah, I understand your question, but wait a minute so I can encrypt my message." Then the patrol called again to say, "We are in the ORP." The commander said, "Okay, I understand. Goodbye."

A patrol can also make different requests of its commander, such as, "I request water." This would simply be stated like:

"Romeo Two-Five this is Romeo Four-Zero, I send Frog Bear, over."

Or, if the patrol were requesting permission to attack an enemy patrol, it would sound like this:

"Romeo Two-Five this is Romeo Four-Zero Mike, I send Goat period. Frog Quail period, over."

The word "period" denotes that there are two sentences in the encrypted message. If you are sending only one sentence, there is no need to use the word "period."

The possible combinations obviously limit message content. However, messages can still contain a considerable amount of information. Be sure to allow the receiving party plenty of time to write down the message by using the "message follows" or "interrogative" warning. Be prepared to repeat the encrypted message.

Encryption of numbers: Numbers can also be encrypted, and this is where the messages can get really complicated. Of course, this is necessary if messages include times, grid locations, numbers of troops, equipment, or casualties.

To encrypt numbers, refer to the section of the SOI marked "Authentication." This includes the digits 1 through 0 matched up to the letters of a ten-character word.

Notice that no letters in the word are repeated. That means, for example, the letter "A" does not appear twice. Of course, you do not have to use an actual word, but using a word makes it easier for the RTO to remember the authentication table. Just use different ten-letter words, like "EXHAUSTION" or "BLACKHORSE" when creating a new SOI.

Example: E X H A U S T I O N
              1 2 3 4 5 6 7 8 9 0

This isn't rocket science. Simply state the letter that corresponds with the number to be encrypted. The number 400 is encrypted on the SOI as "*Alpha November November.*" The time 15:30 is encrypted as "*Echo Uniform Hotel November.*" Get it?

The message "Rendezvous at 14:00 Hours," using the SOI from above, would sound like:

"I send '*Weasel Snapper Echo Alpha November November,*' over."

This relatively short message takes quite a bit of encryption. You can see why you might want to warn the receiver to get a pen and paper to write on. To do this, use the "message follows" statement.

Sender: "Romeo Two-Five, this is Romeo Four-Zero, over."

Receiver: "This is Romeo Two-Five, over."

Sender: "Romeo Two-Five, message follows, over."

Receiver: "Roger Romco Four-Zero, wait one, over. Romeo Four-Zero, this is Romeo Two-Five, send message, over."

This allowed the receiver of the message time to retrieve a pen and paper. The receiver then calls back the sending station and says, "Yeah, what do you want to say?" At that point, the sending station can send their encrypted message.

Authentication: The authentication table is also used to determine whether or not a caller is actually an enemy counter-intelligence operator. Remember that radio waves can be monitored. It is just as easy for the enemy to use an existing call sign and start giving orders or making requests. For example, when an unrecognized caller requests patrol to rendezvous at a road junction, you may be concerned it could be an ambush. Perhaps a station called with a call sign you do recognize, or ordered the patrol to do something that does not make sense. In these cases, demand that the calling station authenticate their possession of the proper SOI.

To do this, simply begin with either a letter *or* a number—it does not matter which. The authenticating station must reply with both the letter *and* number to the immediate left of the number or letter you just stated. So, using the "EXHAUSTION" code listed on the sample SOI, it sounds something like this:

You: "Last calling station, this is Romeo Two-Five, over."

Call Station: "Romeo Two-Five, this is Yankee Nine-Nine, over."

You: "Yankee Nine-Nine, authenticate '*Tango,*' over."

Call Station: "This is Yankee Nine-Nine, I authenticate '*Sierra Six,*' over."

You gave the calling station an authentication start point of "T" on the authentication table. You could have said any available letter or even a number. But, the important thing is the calling station must then authenticate by moving to the immediate left of the letter or number and reading the letter and its corresponding number back. So, the answer "Sierra Six" is correct on this authentication table.

In this case, Yankee Nine-Nine is a legitimate calling station. The reason you do not have that call sign is because Yankee Nine-Nine is not in your company. He may be in another company or may be some kind of support unit, but each unit's SOI should have the same information, except for the call signs. So, Yankee Nine-Nine is holding friendly.

What would have happened if you had given the authentication start point of "Echo?" There is no character to the left of "E" on this particular SOI, so the calling station would have had to move all the way backwards to the end of the table. The correct response would have been "November Zero."

Why authenticate with both the number *and* letter? The enemy is listening and may start to put the code together. A lucky guess is more likely for only one character, but a number/letter combination is much more difficult to guess. The obvious problem is that every time a calling station properly authenticates, it discloses ten percent of its authentication table. This is why you should ask others to authenticate ONLY when you do not recognize their voice or call sign or when the calling station's behavior is irrational or nonsensical, but you will change the SOI at least every twenty-four hours, so the enemy will have little time to break the code.

Realize also that you can change the procedures of the SOI as long as it is standard for the entire team! For instance, you may authenticate to the right instead of the left, or you may get really fancy and only authenticate with letters by counting them two characters back to the left. Any of these procedures are okay, as long as everyone is on the same sheet of music, so to speak.

Passwords: The SOI also includes passwords. Passwords are *not* used over the radio, but are intended for use face-to-face. Furthermore, passwords and running passwords are not used forward of the forward line of troops (FLOT). Forward of the FLOT, each patrol will create their own indigenous number combination to recognize each other, as well as their own unique running password. In this way, the passwords cannot be compromised and used by the enemy to penetrate the lines.

Passwords, then, are used on and behind the FLOT. When a person or group is physically approaching your position, stop them using voice at a distance appropriate to overwhelm them with firepower if necessary. Then, call the person to advance. Give the challenge, and the approaching person must give the correct password. Do not shout the challenge and password! Do it with some discretion. It sounds like this:

You: "Halt. Who is there?"

Person: "I'm Jones from first platoon."

You: "Jones. Advance to be recognized. Red." (The challenge.)

Person: "Smile." (The password.)

You: "Okay, come on in."

If you physically recognize the person, either by sight or sound, you *don't* need to challenge them. Ask who it is in the first place. Once certain they are friendly, allow them to pass through, counting them. If they don't give the password correctly, detain them. They may try to run off, but unless otherwise ordered, only shoot them if they try to attack or push through your position.

The SOI also includes the "running password." It is handled very differently and typically used only after shooting has begun. Running passwords are used when the enemy is chasing a friendly unit. The pointman will yell out the running password as he approaches your position to let you know he is friendly.

THE PHONETIC ALPHABET

Alpha	Bravo	Charlie
Delta	Echo	Fox
Golf	Hotel	India
Juliet	Kilo	Lima
Mike	November	Oscar
Papa	Quebec	Romeo
Sierra	Tango	Uniform
Victor	Whiskey	X-ray
Yankee	Zulu	

COMMON PHRASES

"Over."	— This is the end of my transmission, and I am waiting for your response.
"Out."	— This is the end of my transmission, and no response is required.
"This is . . ."	— I am . . .
"Roger."	— I understand.
"Wilco."	— I will comply.
"Negative."	— No.
"Affirmative."	— Yes.
"Be advised . . ."	— You should be aware that . . .
"Interrogative . . ."	— A question will follow.
"Break."	— I will take a pause and transmit in a few seconds.
"Wait one."	— I will take a pause and transmit in one minute.
"Wait out."	— I will take a pause and transmit in five minutes, or as soon as possible.
"Message follows."	— I will send a message on my NEXT transmission.
"Send message."	— I am prepared to receive your message.
"I send . . ."	— Everything that follows this statement is the message . . .
"How copy."	— Did you successfully receive the message?
"I copy . . ."	— I received the following message . . .
"Correction . . ."	— An error was made and the correct message is . . .
"Say again."	— Repeat our last message.
"I say again . . ."	— I am repeating my last message . . .
"Repeat."	— Fire that exact same *fire mission* again (artillery only).
"Commo check."	— I am requesting a transmission back to my station.
"Negative contact."	— I have received no transmission.
"Last calling station . . ."	— I am addressing the last transmitter of unknown identity . . .
"Authenticate . . ."	— Reference the code book to verify your identity using . . .

Sometimes the pointman will yell out the running password followed by a number, such as "Budweiser Five!" This says there are five people in the friendly patrol. After counting five people running past the position, fire upon any other people running towards the position. Running passwords are used *under fire* or under the pursuit. They are used only forward of the FLOT, such as when a patrol has just departed or is preparing to re-enter the FLOT.

Procedural language: Radio communication carries an established language. These procedural phrases have distinct meanings, and use of these phrases shortens transmission time. It also reduces confusion of communication traffic. All troops should become familiar with these procedural phrases, beginning with the phonetic alphabet.

There is no need to make radio communication difficult or complex. Keep transmissions short and to the point. Do not "talk around" the subject or insert improvised code. This will only confuse matters. Radio communication is never secure, so if vital information cannot be encrypted, try another means of communication. If time is the main factor, send the message over the radio. Be direct and quick.

Shoot, move, and communicate are the basic combat skills. There are numerous communicative systems. Each system has its advantages and disadvantages. Selection of a communication system depends greatly on the needs of the mission. Remember, any communication system can fail. Utilize two or more systems in case the primary communication system fails.

Regarding radio communication language, procedure, and SOI, the best way to learn is to use it! Use the SOI/CEOI in the planning, rehearsals, and execution of each mission. Communication must be protected. Share the SOI with everyone involved in the mission but no one else!

Vocal commands still make up the vast majority of command methods. Direct leaders maintain close contact with their subordinates and guide their actions. Vocal commands and hand and arm signals dominate the battlefield for infantry units.

CHAPTER 2
LEADER SKILLS

TROOP LEADING PROCEDURES

A group is greater than the sum of individual experiences and knowledge. This is called synergy. Synergy achieves exponentially more than individuals working in isolation toward the same goal, but simply placing people together doesn't achieve this synergetic effect. The group must have a single focus, and that focus comes when a leader shares the vision.

Why Use This Procedure?

What follows is a process known as troop leading procedures (TLP). TLP are the means by which a leader shares his vision, formulates a plan, directs the efforts of the group, and continues to supervise all processes. However, TLP are not simply a number of tasks that must be checked off in sequential order. In fact, TLP may not take place in the order given, and often two or more steps will occur concurrently.

Use TLP as a guide through the process of developing the plan and preparing for the mission. Get used to it. Chant these steps until you repeat them in your sleep!

Format
(1) Receive the Mission

Somewhere, somehow, someone will issue the team an order to slay dragons. Yes, the military encourages initiative, but it is unlikely a patrol leader (PL) will ever act upon his own initiative, deciding which mission to undertake. The PL does not determine foreign policy! He waits for orders to come from higher command. That's life.

Leaders project their presence and guidance through troop leading procedures. Never send troops marching without telling them how far to go! The troops want to know what is expected of them even if the news is bad. Let them rise to the occasion.

Upon receiving a mission, conduct analysis with *M*ission, *E*nemy, *T*errain and weather, *T*ime available, *T*roops available, and *C*ivilians on the battlefield (METT-TC). Take notes and ask questions based on the following six questions:

- What's the mission?
- Who's the enemy and what's their disposition?
- Where does the mission take place?
- When does the mission start and end?
- How many troops does the patrol have and how should we coordinate resources?
- Why is this mission important? (This is included in the commander's intent.)

Finally, conduct a preliminary leader's reconnaissance using a topographical map. If there is time for a more in-depth reconnaissance, coordinate it now.

(2) Issue a Warning Order

Immediately after receiving a mission the patrol is informed. They need the information as quickly as possible to begin preparations. Go directly to the troops. Don't pass "go." Don't collect two hundred dollars.

The minimum three requirements of a warning order are:

- The **mission** statement for the element *and* two levels higher,
- The **time** of the operation order, and
- The **place** of the operation order.

Can there be more? Sure! The warning order might be updated upon receiving more information. There's nothing wrong with that. But give the troops the minimum, at least. This will allow them to prepare mentally for the mission, as well as prepare required equipment. It also gives them an idea of how much time they will have for preparation.

(3) Make a Tentative Plan

Now you have to make some decisions, beginning with an estimate of the situation that considers multiple courses of action (COA) and then narrowing that down to one COA. The estimate of the situation is a five-step process:

- Analyze the mission
- Develop multiple COA
- Analyze COA
- Compare COA
- Select COA

Analyze the mission, taking into consideration the mission and intent of the higher commands two levels up. The specified tasks and implied tasks must be identified, and you must look at METT-TC constraints.

When analyzing the time constraints, look at the mission start and end times, then plan backward. If, for example, you know that actions on the objective must be complete at 11:00, then that is a good place to begin backward planning.

1. 11:00 Patrol secures OBJ [**END**]
2. 10:45 Patrol starts actions on OBJ
3. 10:30 Patrol passes through release point
4. 10:10 Patrol departs ORP
5. 10:00 Leader's recon returns to ORP
6. 09:30 Leader's recon departs ORP
7. 09:15 Patrol occupies ORP
8. 08:15 Patrol conducts passage of line through FLOT
9. 08:00 PL links up with FUC/guide
10. 07:45 Patrol occupies AA
11. 07:30 Patrol begins movement to AA
12. 07:15 Leaders conducts PCI
13. 07:00 Patrol conducts rehearsals
14. 06:30 PL issues OPORD
15. 06:00 PL issues WARNO [**START**]

To **develop multiple COA**, consider *O*bservation, *C*over and concealment, *O*bstacles, *K*ey terrain, and *A*venues of approach (OCOKA) and METT-TC again. Taking into effect the enemy's disposition and most likely COA, conduct a risk assessment to (1) identify hazards to the troops, (2) assess the probability of these hazards, and (3) develop controls that eliminate or at least mitigate the risk of those hazards.

Keep the risk assessment in mind when **analyzing the COA**. Look at each COA for its *suitability* to comply with the commander's guidance, its *feasibility* in accomplishing the mission with the resources available, its *acceptability* in terms of cost of resources and casualties, its *"distinguishability"* from other COA, and its *completeness* as a mission statement (the six questions listed previously).

At this point, **compare COA**. At higher levels of command, this is called a "wargame," and it may take hours, weeks, or months. The patrol will have maybe five minutes if very lucky. So, the wargame takes the form of an argument between the PL and the subordinate leaders. Each subordinate leader is encouraged to speak his mind and defend his COA enthusiastically. This helps the PL to see multiple perspectives for each COA.

The last step in making a tentative plan is to **select a COA**. After all arguments, the PL gets the final say.

Remember, this is a tentative plan and isn't etched in stone. However, it gives significant focus to the PL, the subordinate leaders, and the recon team who physically explores the battlefield for feasibility.

(4) Start Movement
Honestly, placing the "start movement" step in the middle of the TLP process never made any sense to me, but I suppose that since movement could occur anywhere in the process, listing it as step four makes as much sense as anywhere else. Just realize that movement can happen at any time in the process.

When the leader says "start movement," that means to move the patrol into an assembly area (AA) just behind the forward line of troops (FLOT), finalize the plans and rehearse.

(*Caution*: The pre-combat inspection [PCI] is conducted prior to movement!)

(5) Conduct Reconnaissance
The recon is an ongoing process as well. For instance, in the step "receive the mission," the PL conducts the minimum form of a leader's recon—a look at the map. Then, as the recon team returns with pertinent information, it might slightly or significantly alter the tentative plan. Heck, it might even cancel the mission entirely!

So, recons are very important to TLP. Reconnaissance may use maps or terrain models, aircraft or high vantage point, or foot patrols. Nowadays, satellite imagery and unmanned aircraft vehicles add to the information. I'd loan you mine, but I'm low on batteries.

(6) Complete the Plan
The PL coordinates with all supporting units, higher command, and the friendly forces to the left, right, and rear of his patrol. (Anything less might result in fratricide!) It is this coordination and the information obtained from the recon that gives the PL the necessary provisions to complete the plan.

With the complete plan in hand, the OPORD is developed. Now remember, it is *not* necessary for the PL to develop the entire OPORD alone. He may task any of the five paragraphs to subordinate leaders *except* the execution paragraph. The leader must create and develop the execution paragraph, which includes the commander's intent and the scheme of fire and maneuver.

(7) Issue the Operation Order
The PL issues the OPORD to the troops. Use a map and overlay, a terrain model, or better yet—stand on the actual terrain of the objective. Again, the only paragraph that the PL is obligated to issue is the execution paragraph. The PL can enlist subordinate leaders to develop and issue the other paragraphs. Be complete, be brief, and be gone!

(8) Supervise the Process
This is another step that is oddly placed because the PL is constantly supervising during TLP. The best plans will fail if competent leaders do not supervise them. A PCI is perhaps the single most important supervisory requirement. Be sure to read that chapter next.

(9) Rehearsals!
Nine steps? Since when did TLP have *nine* steps? Well, if you're planning to fail, TLP has only eight steps. If you plan for victory, then it has nine steps.

Rehearse! I'm begging you—rehearse! No one intentionally makes a stupid plan. Rehearsals show the PL the potential problems in the plan. Every bit as important as this is that rehearsals also allow everyone to see the bigger picture of the operation and exactly how their contributions fit into the scheme of maneuver.

TLP is the process of communicating a vision for task accomplishment, formulating a plan, directing the efforts of the group, and supervising the progress. This is the stuff of history's heroes—seasoned warriors and leaders.

It's worth mentioning that during a study of decision-making involving the leaders of fire departments, the "truth" about critical decision-making was often quite different than the process spelled out in this chapter. More specifically, when time constraints were so severe that critical decisions had to be made within just a few minutes or even seconds, most of this process happened concurrently and not as individual steps.

Furthermore, multiple COA were not considered and assessed. Instead, the first COA that came to the fire captain's mind was issued, and if none of the experienced firemen had any immediate objections, they carried out that COA until it was either successful or proven to be unworkable. In that case, the COA was adjusted on the fly.

What does this mean? It means use the available time to develop the plan, and never become so committed to a plan that you refuse to change, adjust, and adapt if it is clear the plan can no longer accomplish the mission. All plans are tentative. Be flexible.

Combat Orders
Let's talk about your home for a moment. Take a look at the physical structure of it. Now consider the fact that, before your home was built, there was a *need* and a *plan*. This

applies to more than just physical structures. For instance, I'm sure you can think of a sporting event when everything came together brilliantly. I promise you, it wasn't an accident. There was a need and a plan.

Tactics also make use of a need and a plan. The need is called a "purpose" and the plan is called an "order." The purpose is fairly self-explanatory, but more on this later in this chapter. The order gives the patrol the mission, the scheme of maneuver, and the coordinating instructions. There are three types of orders: the warning order (WARNO), the operation order (OPORD), and the fragmentary order (FRAGO).

Why Use This Procedure?

The WARNO serves as a notice of an upcoming mission and OPORD. That seems rather simple, but it's important because it allows troops to prepare mentally and physically. Experienced troops and leaders know from the mission statement what tasks will likely be required. They begin to ready any special equipment in addtion to their standard equipment. The troops also prepare themselves mentally, going over the tasks or lessons learned from previous experience and conducting battle drills or task rehearsals. Finally, the troops can pace themselves to some extent, getting sleep and food prior to the mission.

The OPORD is the detailed plan of the mission, including the scheme of fire and maneuver, and the commander's intent. Obviously, everyone will need to understand what is expected of them, what their specific role is in the mission, and how each troop fits into the "bigger picture." Rehearsals of actions on the objective allow each troop to see that big picture and where everyone will be physically located.

The FRAGO is an adjustment to an existing OPORD. There are many reasons an order might need adjusting. Most commonly, a FRAGO is issued due to a significant change in the situation on the ground or for clarifying instructions.

Format

The following information reflects a generic, standard form for each type of combat order. In many cases, simply cut and paste the information into the format. However, the commander's vision will generate some of this information.

It helps to remember, when developing an order, to think two levels up and plan one level down. That simply means consider the larger operation and its intended effect and then plan fire and maneuvers one echelon lower than your unit. For example, a platoon leader will plan for the fire and maneuvers of his squads while keeping in mind the overall mission of the company and battalion.

At a minimum, the WARNO states the mission, the time of the OPORD, and the place of the OPORD. The WARNO allows subordinate leaders to brief their troops, conduct preparations, and rehearse battle drills that are common to the mission.

WARNO

The warning order allows the troops and element leaders to prepare special equipment unique to a given mission and to begin rehearsals of battle drills and inferred tasks. The WARNO provides answers to the following questions:

- Who is involved in the mission?
- What is the task to be accomplished?
- Why is the patrol performing this mission?
- When is the start time of the OPORD?
- Where is the location of the OPORD?

At a *minimum*, a WARNO includes the following:

- Mission—the task to be accomplished
- Coordinating instructions—the time and location of the OPORD

OPORD

At the risk of sounding irreverent, much of paragraphs 1, 2, 4, and 5 are "cut and paste." (Blasphemy!) Well, probably, but bear with me here. Get the local weather report online, including moonlight and sunlight conditions. Higher command will tell what the mission is, which units will be supporting the mission, and which units will be nearby. Chances are, the patrol already knows its chain of command.

On the other hand, that's simply not the case for Paragraph 3—Execution. Nope, this paragraph requires the troops to use their heads for something other than a nifty place to display fashionable head gear!

Every mission deserves a well-thought-out plan! The five paragraphs of an OPORD develop that plan and issue it in a standardized format. Repeated use of this format allows the team to orient on key information to see the big picture.

The commander issues the OPORD and orients the OPORD to the terrain. Ideally, he gives the order while standing on the terrain. This may be possible in the case of the defense, but it is highly unlikely for any other type of combat operation. In those cases, he uses a terrain model or topographical map.

Paragraph 3a—Concept of the Operation—is the very heart of the OPORD because it details the overall scheme of fire and maneuver. That's the real heart of the matter, right? It answers the question, "*How* to achieve this?"

The commander's intent is the soul of the operation. The commander's intent answers the questions, "*What* are we going to do, and *why* are we doing this?" This is the most critical information of any mission—what, why, and how.

Through the **commander's intent** statement, the commander explains in very concise terms what it is he expects to achieve. Believe it or not, there is an art to this statement because it includes subtle nuances that every troop must understand.

In essence, the commander's intent statement includes three concerns—the purpose, key tasks, and an end state. The purpose explains why this mission is important. The key tasks are those tasks and/or conditions that must be met to achieve success. The end state is a description of how the commander envisions success.

Amazingly, all of this must occur in three sentences. Yep. That's it—three! After you've stated your commander's intent, the lowest ranking troop on the mission must be able to repeat it perfectly. If the lowest ranking troop can't do this, your commander's intent statement is *too long*! Shorten it.

Be concise. The **purpose** is direct. For example, "Friendly supply convoys must use this highway." That's direct, unambiguous information.

The **key tasks** describe *conditions*. *Don't* assign tasks to specific units or individuals. DON'T assign specific equipment to achieve the task. *Don't* assign time hacks. *Don't* assess risks. If you do these things, you aren't giving the troops what they need—a description of the conditions for success! For example, "We will control the ridgelines on both sides of the highway to prevent the enemy from firing at our convoys." Okay, controlling the ridgeline is a condition, or key task.

The **end state** is a description of how the commander envisions a successful outcome. For example, "Success comes when the last of the four convoys pass through our valley undamaged."

That's three concise sentences and a clear commander's intent statement:

"Friendly supply convoys must use this highway. We will control the ridgelines on both sides of the highway to prevent the enemy from firing at our convoys. Success comes when the last of the four convoys pass through our valley undamaged."

Anything longer is too much.

Q: Why is the commander's intent statement so important?
A: Because it allows subordinate leaders to accomplish the mission even if the original order cannot be carried out as planned. In short, it allows for individual initiative.

Paragraph 1—*SITUATION*
  a. Enemy forces and battlefield conditions
    1. Weather and sunlight/moonlight data
    2. Terrain, using factors of OCOKA
    3. Enemy forces
      Uniform identification
      Unit identification
      Recent activities
      Strengths/weaknesses
      Current location
      Most probable COA

b. Friendly forces

   1. The larger unit's mission and commander's intent

   2. Adjacent unit missions and locations

   3. Fire support unit identification

   4. Other supporting unit identification

Paragraph 2—*MISSION*

   Identify the task to be completed by *this* unit

Paragraph 3—*EXECUTION*

   Commander's Intent

   Purpose

   Key Tasks

   End State

   a. Concept of the operation

      1. Scheme of maneuver

      2. Fire

      3. Engineer support

   b. Tasks to maneuver units

      1. Task for each element

      2. Purpose for each element

   c. Tasks to combat support units

   d. Coordinating instructions

      1. Movement instructions

         SP time and location

         Order of march

         Route of march

         Rendezvous time and location (AA, ERP, ORP)

         LOA and PL

      2. Passage of lines

         Linkup time and location

         Passage point location

      3. Priority intelligence requirements (PIR)

      4. Troop safety

         RFL and weapons control status

Paragraph 4—*SERVICE SUPPORT* [or *ADMINISTRATION and LOGISTICS*]

   a. Concept of support

      Location of combat field supply

      Location of aid station

      Scheme of support

   b. Material and services

      1. Supply

      2. Transportation

      3. Service

      4. Maintenance

   c. Medical evacuation procedures

   d. Coordination for civilian personnel and EPW

Paragraph 5—*COMMAND and SIGNAL*

   a. Command

      1. Location of leaders

      2. Succession of command

   b. Signal

      1. SOI/CEOI in effect

      2. Radio communications restrictions

         Listening silence and time frame

         Alternate frequencies and conditions for frequency change

      3. Visual and pyrotechnic signals

      4. Brevity codes specific to the operation

      6. Electronic protection, including COMSEC guidelines and procedures

Before the OPORD can be issued, some type of orientation device must be identified or created. A map will do, but a terrain model is much better at conveying the lay of the land. Terrain models can be made with simple material—tape, string, and stones.

Rehearse! Rehearse! Rehearse! Conduct yourself in battle exactly as you conduct yourself in training. Rehearsals allow troops to see how they fit into the bigger picture of the mission. And, they allow troops to see any glaring mistakes before they're made!

FRAGO

Fragmentary orders adjust the mission from the current OPORD. As such, this information depends on the specifics of the tactical situation. FRAGO may include:

- Updates to the enemy or friendly situation
- Changes to the scheme of maneuver
- Coordinating and clarifying instructions
- Expanding the mission tasks (branches and sequels)

Every worthwhile endeavor in life requires a need and a plan. Combat orders spell out the need and plan. The WARNO informs troops of an upcoming mission. The OPORD goes into great detail and, most significantly, includes the commander's intent and the scheme of the operation's fire and maneuvers—the what, why, and how. The FRAGO allows the commander to adjust the mission once the OPORD has been issued.

As a practical matter, too much information is a bad thing. Conversely, more information is always good. Both of these statements are correct. It's a paradox. While it is true that more information is good because an informed troop possesses the essential situational awareness to be successful on the battlefield, it is also true that information is not the rarest commodity. In fact, *attention span* is the rarest commodity!

Keep this in mind as you consider that, typically, a squad leader has about fifteen minutes to issue the OPORD to his or her squad. If they are very lucky, they might get another ten minutes to run through a shoulder-to-shoulder rehearsal. Now, of course, the U.S. Army's Ranger School Cadre would have me burned at the stake for such a heretical statement because even the squad and platoon OPORD is allotted a full two hours to issue and an additional hour of walk-crawl-run rehearsal time. (Roll eyes upward.)

While I'd argue that a three-hour OPORD is fairly common at the company level, I've rarely ever seen such a thing at the platoon and squad level. It is a rare thing indeed. So, realize that time plays a major factor in issuing the OPORD. If you have a great deal of time to issue this order, then by all means give copious amounts of information to the troops! If on the other hand, you have just fifteen minutes, give only the most essential information. After all, the troops really don't care that the moonrise will be at 02:12 if the forecast says cloudy and rain all night long! Don't attempt to dazzle the troops with useless information, or I promise you, they'll be as lost as last year's Easter egg.

PRE-COMBAT INSPECTION

Rarely does a mission fail due to a bad plan. I'm not saying that good tactics are unimportant. However, the process of developing an operation order (OPORD) through troop leading procedures (TLP) guides the patrol leader (PL) in the design of a plan. In short, recognize a stupid plan early on in the process.

So, why do missions fail? Usually, because they lack:

1. Pre-combat inspection (PCI)
2. Commander's intent
3. Rehearsals

Why Use This Procedure?

The PCI is a stopgap—protection from failure. How many times have you been out on a mission only to discover a member of the patrol has forgotten an essential piece of equipment, or worn brand new boots, or has a weapon malfunction? How many times have you returned from a mission to hear troops complain they didn't understand what they were trying to achieve? Right. It's common—far too common.

Skipping the PCI is the wrong way to conduct operations. The PCI is absolutely essential in that it checks:

1. Each troop's equipment necessary for mission accomplishment
2. Each troop's understanding of the mission purpose (commander's intent)
3. Each troop's understanding of how his or her task contributes to the mission

That means the PCI looks at equipment, asks questions regarding the commander's intent, and asks questions regarding the rehearsal. In this manner, the PCI guards against missing any of these critical TLP steps.

(*Caution*: The PCI is typically conducted in *two stages!* Subordinate leaders conduct the first PCI prior to movement to the AA. They inspect equipment only. The PL conducts the second PCI immediately after the rehearsal. The PL inspects equipment and mission knowledge.)

Format

The PCI is best achieved with a checklist. This keeps troops from missing important key equipment and situational awareness. Mark this page as a checklist or simply copy the following information to a note card and carry it with you.

Equipment

Troops are inspected for what to bring and what *not* to bring. This will differ greatly depending on their role in the patrol. Every infantry unit must be able to shoot, move, and communicate. Those are the three basic infantry skills. The PCI makes sure that each troop can do this.

Uniform and Gear:

- Check that the troop is wearing the proper uniform and camouflage
- Check that boots are serviceable, comfortable, and appropriate
- Check that rain and cold-weather gear is carried if needed
- Check water canteens and bladders are full and the troop is hydrated
- Check that first-aid kits are present and complete

Something as simple as an empty canteen, dead battery, or missing rain parka can doom a patrol to failure. Subordinate leaders *must* conduct an inspection of their troops prior to each combat mission! Troops invariably try to carry too much or too little.

- Check that ID tags are worn, as well as special medical tags (allergies)
- Check that all specialty equipment is carried in either the LBE or rucksack
- Check all leaders for appropriate maps and compass/GPS
- Check all leaders for communication devices
- Check for secured gear by having the troop jump up and down

Communication Devices:
- Check that extra batteries, antenna, mic, and basic radio kit are present
- Check that the radio is set to the proper channel and/or frequency
- Check the SOI/CEOI and ensure that each troop knows the call signs and code
- Check that all field phones are serviceable, clean, and in watertight containers
- Check for whistles, flares, color panels, and other communication devices.

Weapon Systems:
- Check that each weapon system is assigned to the appropriate troop
- Check that each weapon is serviceable, clean, and zeroed
- Check that ammunition is serviceable and plentiful for each weapon
- Check that lubrication is present, as well as field cleaning kits
- Check optical devices (day and night) are serviceable
- Check that extra batteries are carried for optical devices

Specialty Equipment:
- Check for first-aid kits
- Check for protective gear—body armor, eye wear, kneepads, etc.
- Check for screening smoke canisters
- Check for wire breaching/marking equipment, if appropriate
- Check for mines/explosives if appropriate
- Check for anti-armor weapons if appropriate
- Check for rappelling/climbing/crossing gear, if appropriate
- Check for pioneering tools if appropriate

MISSION KNOWLEDGE

Frankly speaking, there is very little point in venturing forth on a mission if troops haven't been informed about what they're doing or trying to achieve. You might have the best plan in the world, but it won't do any good if that plan hasn't been shared!

Conversely, even a mediocre plan can succeed if everyone understands the plan and works toward its accomplishment.

Commander's Intent:
- Check that each troop understands the mission purpose
- Check that each troop understands the key tasks he must achieve
- Check that each troop understands the end state of success

Rehearsal:
- Check that each troop understands the mission statement
- Check that each troop understands assigned task(s)
- Check that each troop knows how to identify the enemy
- Check that each troop knows the expected light, weather, and terrain conditions
- Check that each troop knows where other friendly troops are located
- Check that each troop knows his leader and SOI/CEOI information

Mission failures due to equipment malfunction or a lack of mission knowledge are completely preventable! A single item can doom the mission. For example, if the temperature drops and it begins to rain, a troop without a rain parka quickly slips into hypothermia. The troop becomes a weather casualty and has to be evacuated, which delays the mission, and the evacuation process might disclose the patrol position and eliminate the element of surprise. That can mean deadly consequences.

Avoid this nonsense! Be a responsible leader and conduct PCI. It takes only a few minutes to do this. Have subordinate leaders check each troop's equipment and specialty equipment prior to moving to the AA. After rehearsals are conducted, check the equipment a second time, and check each troop's knowledge of the mission.

AFTER-ACTION REVIEW

After victory or failure, there is only one way to learn—talk about it. Remember, the battlefield is a dynamic place. Constant change means whichever opponent adapts quicker, wins the battle.

People tell stories for many reasons. One reason is to assess a practice or policy. That is what an after-action review (AAR) really is. It's a series of stories evaluating policies and practices unique to that mission and particular set of circumstances.

Regardless of who actually conducts the AAR, the leader's role is to listen to the story, evaluate the mission, and plan for future training and missions. Depending on the culture of the team, this may be difficult for some leaders to sit through. People often invest their egos as leaders, and when it comes to finger-pointing, the leader is often the most visible and easiest to blame. Nonetheless, when both team and leader internalize the AAR process, this group exploration is perhaps the most powerful tool for the development of the team's skills!

Why Use This Procedure?

The AAR is a tool that allows team members to explore causes of gaps between the plan and the performance. However, the AAR is more than a debriefing. A debrief simply gives information. The AAR is an exploratory exercise whereby the effort is to get the team members to reach conclusions on their own—to internalize the solution to the problem as well as the AAR process itself.

Format

Moderating the AAR is conducted in four logical steps:

    The Plan
    The Performance
    The Issues
    The Fix

The Plan

This phase details "what was supposed to happen." In fact, it is nothing more than a restatement of the operation order (OPORD) in a concise form. The patrol leader (PL) will stand in front of the team and quickly restate the commander's intent and the scheme of maneuver.

Remember this is not "what I think *might* have happened" or "what I really *wished* had happened." There should be no conjecture or grandstanding at this point. It's simply a restatement of the plan.

The Performance

The second phase of the AAR details "what really happened." Those team members who were on the ground taking part in the action state this part of the AAR. The PL is generally discouraged from speaking during this phase without a unique perspective or useful information.

Egos should not be on the line taking up time arguing or finger pointing, but leadership needs a realistic measure of performance. This can be a painful, embarrassing process, but remember, people don't make stupid plans. If the plan was stupid, the planning phase usually catches it. So, why didn't the mission go off just as planned? Or did it? The AAR looks for the gap between the plan and the actual performance.

The AAR allows the team to learn from battlefield experiences. At its very core, the AAR identifies the issues that create a gap between the plan and the performance. Once these issues are known, correct any deficiencies.

The Issues

Once you've established the gap between the plan and the performance, set out to identify the reasons for the discrepancy. In truth, command and troops usually stumble across and identify the issues during the performance phase. However, it will be necessary to restate these issues so everyone can see the big picture. This responsibility typically falls to the observer-controller during training but may be executed by the PL in lieu of an observer.

The Fix

The last step of the AAR is to identify who—by name—is responsible for correcting the deficiencies contributing to the gap between the plan and the performance. Do not assume all the responsibility falls to the PL. Subordinate leaders and even experienced troops can lead training or take responsibility for equipment operation/procurement. The PL assigns these tasks accordingly.

Moderating: Ideally, an outside source, such as an observer/controller, conducts the AAR. If there is no outside source, the PL moderates the AAR. Use a representation of the terrain covered in the mission. This can be a terrain model, a map, or even video and photographs of the mission. The point is to get everyone thinking on the same sheet of music.

The key to managing the AAR is to moderate the flow of communication. Don't control it so much that people hesitate to give valuable insight. On the other hand, many troops see the AAR as a chest-thumping exercise and drone on

LEADER SKILLS

incessantly about "who killed whom." Enthusiasm is good, but don't get lost in bravado.

The moderator must persuade the troops to hold off on war stories until later, when everyone has a beer in them. This is no easy task when you consider the material at hand. The troops will be fresh from the fight. If the mission went well, you can bet there will be a great deal of bragging. If the mission did not go as well, finger-pointing begins even before the AAR. These explosive moments of temper or praise may be justified, but that is not the AAR objective.

Be sure to include everyone's perspective. It is customary to begin with the element leaders because they typically have the best vantage points. However, it is important to ask even the basic rifleman to speak because, often, the crucial moment between success and failure is witnessed not by some high-ranking commander but by a common foot soldier.

For the first phase, **the plan**, it is a good idea to begin an AAR by asking each of the element leaders what mission they were tasked to do and to let them answer in their own words. A good leader listens to the clarity of focus from each of these subordinate leaders for their grasp of the mission as a whole and the understanding of their element's role in the mission.

For the second phase, **the performance**, the initial movement is a good place to start within the execution of the mission. Did the patrol hit their start time? How about the time hacks for phase lines or reaching their objective rally point (ORP)? If not, this may explain any "accordion" effect in the time frames or the physical movement of the formation.

Actions in the ORP must be addressed. Was a leader's recon forward of the ORP required? Were the plans finalized in the ORP and, if so, did the leaders feel confident that the members of their elements understood these plans? Often, when plans are changed in the ORP, the lines of communication have gaps. Only with clearly delineated responsibilities and element integrity can these communication barriers be overcome.

Actions on the objective (OBJ) include all considerations from the release point—that magical place on the map where the commander relinquishes control to subordinate leaders—up to the point of reconsolidation. To list every consideration would be too much information for this single chapter, but most issues fall within each element's ability to "shoot, move, and communicate." More exactly, this refers to the ability of each element to engage the enemy within their sectors of fire, to move toward and across the OBJ, and to coordinate these efforts with friendly elements to their flanks and rear. Most of the AAR is spent focusing on the actions on the OBJ and with good reason. It is on the objective that all efforts are either realized in success or lost in defeat.

Identify **the issues** in the third phase. It is a good idea to allow some venting—whether negative or positive—because everyone wants his "day in court," so to speak. By this, I mean troops will volunteer to suppress their impulse to lay blame or give praise long enough for the AAR to be fruitful. Also, they may be intelligent enough to know that they should listen to the other side (or sides) of the story before they go about making accusations. However, troops will only do so if they have reason to believe that they will eventually be able to voice their opinions and concerns. So, even though a moderator may lose some control of the flow of information, it is a good idea to invite everyone to speak his mind during this phase.

There is a little technique that I have found works. The "nut shelling" technique requires everyone to make a concise statement on the exercise, though, under tactical constraints, there is usually little time for such niceties. To begin, simply single out the most vocal member of the group and ask him what needs to be the focus of future training, or more simply, what was the most significant thing to go wrong with the mission? Then ask the next troop what one thing they saw that was well-executed or coordinated. Move around the group, alternating these two simple questions back and forth. Listen closely for consensus on these areas. A neat variation of this technique is to make those troops most vocal about negative issues give a positive observation of the mission and to ask the most positive troops to give a negative observation of the mission.

Finally, before the AAR draws to a close, identify those individuals who will be responsible for **the fix** of each issue. Often, this means an individual is assigned a leadership role in training the troops on the identified task or deficiency. Just as common is to fix or acquire necessary equipment. Sometimes, a fix simply means to research the problem and report back to the team and/or leaders with the findings.

Don't forget to discuss success as well. The one way to be sure that troops will continue to execute tasks correctly is to *tell them* when they are right!

At the very minimum, leaders are expected to walk away from the AAR understanding the sentiment of the troops. This should not be taken lightly. The troops' needs and concerns should be addressed as soon as possible— most importantly, those resources a commander can give his troops immediately, such as more detailed combat orders and coordination between elements. The AAR helps gather the information necessary to meet these needs.

SECTION 2
TEAM BATTLE DRILLS

"Where we go one, we go all!" Battle drills are executed with scarce time to assess the situation or coordinate a response. The drill is executed in perfect order, as it has been rehearsed time and time again. Precision and violence are its momentum.

CHAPTER 3
SECURITY POSTURES

MOVEMENT TECHNIQUES

It's time to discuss how to move a patrol from point A to point B. The techniques used would be better described as methods of security while traveling, but that's a mouthful. Instead, these are **movement techniques**.

Keep in mind that movement techniques are not formations. These techniques are used with *any* of the attack formations. Essentially, movement techniques are concerned with the distances between troops and units while traveling. The critical factor of any movement technique is that the patrol leader be able to see the subordinate leaders and vice-versa because most of the communication and coordination is through hand and arm signals.

Additionally, subordinate elements should not become so spread apart they can no longer support each other. Weapon systems have finite ranges. Rugged terrain and heavy vegetation limit weapon systems. In these cases, the distances between subordinate elements should be even less.

Why Use This Drill?

The first technique, known as the **traveling technique**, is used primarily for walking a patrol down a road or path in fairly secured areas. Use the traveling technique when enemy contact is *unlikely*.

The second technique, known as the **traveling overwatch**, is the most common technique employed when moving troops in unsecured areas. Use the traveling overwatch when enemy contact is *likely*.

The third technique, known as the **bounding overwatch**, is the preferred technique when security is the most important factor. Use the bounding overwatch when enemy contact is *expected*.

Decision Points

In the business world, it is commonly said a product or service can be fast, cheap, or good. Indeed, a product can be a combination of any two, but not all three! If a product is fast and cheap, its quality is compromised, so it's not very "good." If a product is cheap and good, it will take a long time to achieve, so it's not very "fast." If a product is fast and good, it will take many skilled laborers to produce it, so it will not be "cheap."

In a very similar manner, the PL considers factors of speed, control, and security. So, while the bounding overwatch offers excellent control and security, it is notoriously slow. On the other end of the spectrum is the traveling technique, which maintains top speed and control but dangerously lacks security! Somewhere in the middle is the traveling overwatch, which offers adequate speed and security but significantly compromises the PL's control.

Keeping this in mind, the PL assesses the situation to determine the emphasis on speed, control, and security. In essence, the PL considers the appropriate distance between troops and subordinate elements.

Many issues factor into this consideration. Are the troops moving in their own secured area? Are they crossing rough or heavily vegetated terrain? Are they moving in nighttime or daytime light conditions? How soon do they need to be at the destination? How many troops are moving—a fairly large unit or a smaller one?

The most important consideration the PL takes into account is whether or not enemy contact is unlikely, likely, or expected.

Contrary to popular myth, troops do use roads to travel. In most cases, it is not only acceptable but also the most efficient means of travel. However, certain techniques mitigate the potential danger of attack while moving along roads. Use the traveling formation when enemy contact is possible.

Take Action!

The goal of movement technique is to get the troops from one point to another safely. Contrary to popular opinion, this should not require any running, unless under fire. If the troops are running, someone has done a very poor job of planning!

What should also be obvious is that each technique allows for defensive fire in reaction to the enemy. The PL must consider the coordination of this fire in the planning phase.

Traveling Technique

1. The patrol is massed together as one entity for ease of command, control, and communication (C3). This technique allows for speed of movement.
2. Troops are spaced five meters apart. If marching on a road, two lines are formed with troops staggered left and right. This creates a distance of ten meters between the troops on one side of the road, but still only five meters behind or in front of the troop to the opposite side of the road.
3. The patrol disperses to the left and right in the event of attack. This technique permits very little deterrence to the effectiveness of mass-casualty-producing weapons but does concentrate the troops for a massed assault in the event of a near ambush.

Traveling Overwatch

1. The patrol is separated into two or more elements. This technique is also fast. It has considerably more security and flexibility for each element to maneuver in support of another if attacked. However, the PL loses some of the control in that each element is now commanded by a subordinate leader. The PL maintains contact with these leaders.
2. There are still five meters between troop, and the troops are staggered in two lines when roads are used. However, a distance of *at least* twenty meters is maintained between each element.
3. The patrol disperses left and right in the event of attack. This technique has improved security in its ability to deter the effect of mass-casualty-producing weapons and has further advantages in regard to its ability to disperse and overwhelm a near or far ambush.

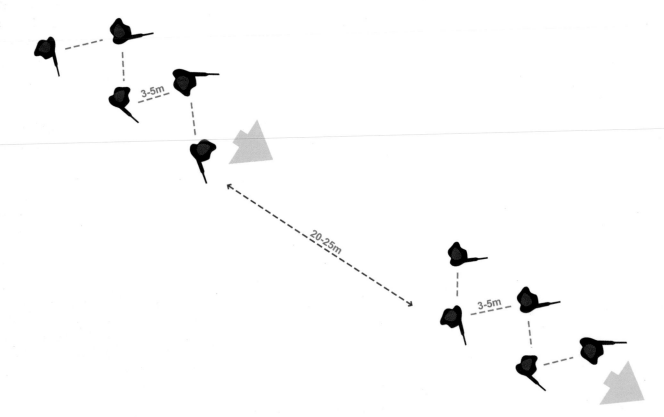

Use the traveling overwatch formation when enemy contact is likely. The traveling overwatch separates each element by about twenty-five meters so it is difficult for the enemy to attack the entire patrol at once.

Bounding Overwatch

1. The patrol is separated into exactly two elements, though there is no requirement for these elements to be equal in size. This technique compromises speed for greater security and control.

2. The forward element halts in a position that offers the best observation of the terrain in front of the patrol. This element becomes the "overwatch" position. The position must offer some cover or concealment.

3. The trail element (behind the forward element) then bounds forward, either slightly left or right of the overwatch position. This bounding element uses a route that:

   • Offers the most concealment
   • Does *not* mask the fire of the overwatch position
   • Does *not* exceed the supportive fire range of the overwatch position

4. Once the bounding element has successfully passed through the terrain, they take up a position that offers the best observation of the terrain in front of them. The bounding element now becomes the overwatch position and the old overwatch bounds forward.

5. This process is repeated until the patrol reaches its objective, or the PL selects another movement technique due to an improved security situation. Movement is very slow, and stealth is preferred rather than a noisy, clumsy rush. In short, don't run unless fired upon or ordered to do so!

Use the bounding overwatch technique when enemy contact is expected. The effort is to make maximum use of combat power in the direction of movement, while presenting any potential enemy observation with the smallest force exposed.

6. If the patrol comes under fire, the bounding overwatch becomes quick and violent. The overwatch position conducts suppressive fire while the PL directs the bounding element to either conduct a hasty attack against the enemy or break contact.

Troops must move. That's the nature of warfare. The trick here is to employ the technique appropriate to the present level of danger. Remember, contact with the enemy is either *unlikely*, *likely*, or *expected*.

It is unrealistic to assume troops will always move with the highest level of security, the bounding overwatch. The troops become easily fatigued, and movement is slowed unreasonably. Conversely, it's unrealistic to assume troops will always use the least amount of security, the traveling technique, in order to capitalize on speed. Such a practice eventually results in a disastrous meeting with the enemy!

The PL chooses the appropriate technique for the given situation. Subordinate leaders enforce strict adherence to the assigned interval distances between troops and elements.

Remember that, once again, supporting fire covers the distance between troops and elements. That is, the different elements employing the traveling techniques must be able to fire in support of each other. Since most paintball and airsoft systems have a practical range of sixty meters, at distances greater than sixty meters the elements can no longer support each other.

ATTACK FORMATIONS

Yeah! Finally, some action! Here's critical information you can put to work immediately. At this point, I should require that you demonstrate the infantryman's super-secret handshake, but if you'll excuse the breach of etiquette, we can skip the formalities.

This chapter discusses the three most common attack formations—the column, the line, and the wedge. Additionally, we'll take a look at a couple of variations, including the diamond and the staggered column.

Keep in mind that these formations are building blocks for the entire element. What that means is that the smallest element, the fireteam, may be in a wedge while the larger element, such as the squad or platoon, may be in another formation. It is quite possible to have fireteams in wedges, squads in columns, and the platoon in line—all at the same time! Confused? Don't worry, I'll explain.

Why Use This Drill?

Attack formations are just that, formations in the traditional sense of armed combat. They are designed to allow the maximum use of weaponry, while limiting the patrol's exposure to the enemy. The beauty of each of these formations is their simplicity. Every troop in the formation knows their sector of fire simply by where they are positioned in the formation. Command and control (C2) of attack formations can be a challenge, but when implemented correctly, these formations allow for adequate flow of communication.

Decision Points

So which formation to choose? Once again, this decision is very much the art of war. Each formation has distinct advantages and disadvantages. The PL selection depends greatly on the situation and, more specifically, on the enemy threat, terrain, light conditions, ease of communication, and—most importantly—intended effect upon the enemy.

The decision comes down to four considerations that exclude each other to an extent. Those considerations include:

- C2
- Maneuverability
- Firepower forward
- Protection of the flanks

The Line

The line formation places excellent firepower forward, employing virtually one hundred percent of the unit's weapon systems to the front. Additionally, C2 is easily achieved along a line formation, making the line an excellent choice for frontal assaults against the enemy!

The disadvantages include a lack of maneuverability and an almost complete inability to protect the flank. Regardless of the interval distance between each troop in the line formation, they are literally lined up in a side-by-side fashion. This means only the last troop on either flank can engage an enemy force to the sides of this formation. If any other friendly troop attempted to do this, they would literally be firing right past or *through* their own troops! This means that the line formation is incredibly vulnerable to enemy fire from the flanks.

Also, for the line formation to change directions is practically impossible. This requires that one troop act as the pivot point, while the other troops hurry along in an effort to stay online and not mask anyone else's sector of fire. For those troops on the far flank from the pivot, this maneuver becomes a living hell as they run at top speeds across the battlefield, exposed to enemy fire. In short, the line cannot turn.

Create the line formation by standing abreast of each other with key leaders situated just behind or to the immediate flank of the formation. This formation is effective for making sweeps through open terrain with expected enemy fire superiority.

The Column File

The column file formation scores high in three areas. It lends great ease of C2, maneuvers almost as easily as the individual troop, and can employ virtually every weapon to either flank. There is little doubt the column file is the infantryman's favorite formation and, for better or for worse, it is by far the most common!

The column file is an excellent choice for moving through difficult terrain. Because C2 is communicated so easily, the column file is also ideal for moving in times of limited visibility, such as nighttime. In battle, the column file also has advantages. Contrary to popular myth, the column file is a difficult formation to ambush because it permits the use of virtually every single weapon system to either flank! Additionally, this formation is ideal for penetrating or flanking an enemy position because, as the column comes perpendicular to the enemy position, a simple left or right turn allows every troop to employ his or her weapon against the enemy. In this case, the column file simply transforms into a line formation, which is excellent for attacking forward.

The single disadvantage of the column formation is its inability to place adequate fire forward or backward of the formation. Troops behind the point man cannot fire forward without hitting their own troops! If the enemy is able to place significant fire upon the column formation, this can prove to be disastrous.

The Wedge

The wedge formation seems to be the compromise between the line and column formations. The wedge formation scores high in terms of firepower forward and protection of the flanks. It also scores moderately in maneuverability.

Using the wedge formation, the patrol can still employ almost all weapons forward against an enemy force. Additionally, since about half of all weapons can be instantly brought to bear to either flank, this formation proves to be very difficult to ambush or flank! While pivoting the formation is a bit difficult—especially in steep or heavily vegetated terrain—it is far easier to maneuver the wedge than the line formation.

The wedge has a considerable disadvantage in its inability to communicate C2 up and down the formation. To do so would require the troops to constantly look inward and backward along the formation instead of into the assigned sectors of fire. This would negate any advantages the wedge had in firepower or maneuverability! A troop simply cannot simultaneously look inward and outward of the formation, move with stealth, and communicate with multiple element leaders. It's ridiculous to think so, and the consequence is that C2 is compromised, which ironically places greater emphasis on subordinate leaders to control the formation and maneuverability. In darkness or challenging terrain, this quickly becomes exhausting!

Form the column formation with each troop following behind the point man like ducks in a row. These "ducks" have impressive weaponry and a primary sector of observation alternating left and right down the line. The drag man watches rearward.

The wedge formation with the lead troop forward and each subsequent troop assuming a position to the left and right as the formation recesses. The wedge permits excellent firepower forward and to either flank. Shown is a column of wedges.

Take Action!

Similar to the movement techniques, attack formations do *not* necessarily require running. A common misconception is that because the patrol is in a formation in which it clearly expects enemy contact, the patrol is instantly committed to rushing forward in a loud, clumsy manner. This is simply not the case.

Each formation offers distinct advantages over the other, and employing the right formation for the situation allows the patrol to be very aggressive. However, stealth is still the preferred mode of operation, getting close to the enemy without giving the enemy the advantage of their standoff weaponry. Why rush through 400 meters of enemy machine-gun fire if you can maneuver to just 20 meters from that machine-gun position and attack across a very short distance?

The Column File

1. This formation is constructed by having each troop follow the point man in single file. Yes, this formation looks just like the lunch line at school.
2. The point man's sector of fire is the 120-degree field of view to his front. The second man in line must monitor a 90-degree sector of fire to the left of the formation. The third man in the line must monitor a 90-degree sector of fire to the right of the formation, and so on. The sectors of fire are staggered left and right for every member of the patrol except the drag man. The drag man's sector of fire is a 120-degree field of view to the rear of the formation.
3. Hand and arm signals are the preferred method of communication. Communication is passed up and down the formation. This means that *every sixth step* of the left foot, each troop should *turn around* to see if any information is being passed UP the column formation!
4. When any one member of the formation stops, every member halts. Typically, each member takes a knee upon the formation's halt. After three minutes, each patrol member takes a couple of steps in the direction they are facing (their sector of fire). This clears the center path for leaders and key teams to use. After five minutes, each patrol member drops his or her rucksack and assumes a prone position until the signal to move out is given.

The column formation allows the best command and control of troops. It is also the easiest formation to maneuver. While it has ample security to the flanks, it makes poor use of combat power forward and to the rear, where it is very vulnerable.

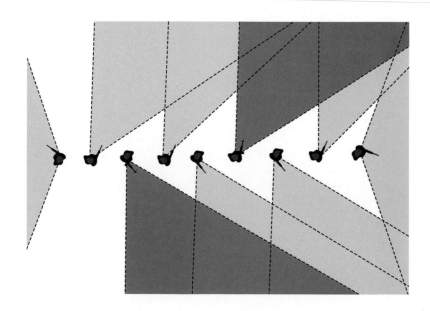

Variation: The Staggered Column. When the patrol uses a road or developed path, they will form two lines, one on each side of the road. This is achieved by alternately assuming a position based on the opposite side of the road from the man in front of you. More simply, if the point man takes the left side, the next troop takes the right, and the next troop takes the left, and so on. This forms two columns—one to the right side of the road and one to the left side of the road. Otherwise, the staggered column functions exactly like the column file.

The Line

1. All troops are formed into a rank, side by side. Each troop faces forward and has essentially a 90-degree sector of fire. Subordinate leaders maintain control over the formation, being careful not to allow any portion of the line formation to get ahead of the others. This could risk fratricide or, at the very least, mask the fire of friendly troops.
2. Hand and arm signals are the preferred method of communication and should be passed left and right along the formation. This means that *every sixth step* of the left foot, each troop should *look left and right* to see if any information is being passed along the line formation.
3. When any one member of the formation stops, every member halts. Each member takes a knee upon the formation's halt, facing forward. The troops on the far left and right face out accordingly. After five minutes, each patrol member drops his or her rucksack and assumes a prone position until the signal to move out is given.

The Wedge

1. This formation is constructed by offsetting each troop to the left and right of the point man. This forms a wide, inverted "V."
2. The point man's sector of fire is, again, the 120-degree field of view to his front. The next two members in the formation, behind the point man's position and offset to the left and right, monitor a 90-degree sector of fire that begins directly forward and covers their immediate left or right, respectively. This is also true for the last troop in the formation, being offset one more time to the left or right of the troop in front of him. There is no rear sector of fire because subsequent fireteams follow behind.
3. Hand and arm signals are the preferred method of passing communication up and down the formation. This means that *every sixth step* of the left foot, each troop should *turn inward* to see if any information is being passed along the wedge formation.
4. While it is acceptable to temporarily halt the wedge formation—in which each troop takes a knee—it is inadvisable to halt troops for any length of time in this formation. That is because C2 is very difficult to achieve, and soon troops and subordinate leaders lose situational awareness. That's dangerous. If a long stop is required, the PL designates another attack formation before halting the patrol, or the PL rallies the patrol into a security halt.

The wedge formation can configure a series of wedges to form on line, in column, or even in wedge. Fireteams in wedge with the squad in wedge (when three fireteams are used) makes maximum use of the squad's firepower forward and to the flanks.

There are many types of danger areas—large and small. Inevitably, the linear danger area is the most common. These include roads, paths, creeks, rivers, tree lines, fences, and alleyways. For every danger area, there is a method for crossing.

Variation: The Diamond. The diamond formation, also known as the "modified wedge," is an acceptable alternative to the wedge. If there are four members of the fire team, simply place the fourth troop, last in line, directly behind the point man. If there are five members of the fireteam, place the fireteam leader in the very middle of the formation in line with the point man and drag man.

Be warned that the diamond formation will not allow a maximum deployment of the fireteam's weaponry against targets forward of the patrol. However, it still allows an acceptable percentage of the weapons to be brought to bear against an enemy force in front and to the flanks of the formation. The trade-off is that, with the diamond formation, the fireteam may move with more speed, change directions with more ease, and provide 360 degrees of security for itself.

Attack formations are designed to allow the maximum use of weaponry while limiting the patrol's exposure to the enemy. Every troop knows his sector of fire according to his position within the formation. The PL selects the appropriate formation based on C2, maneuverability, firepower forward, and protection of the formation's flanks.

Each tactical situation is unique and not restricted to just one formation or another. Employ all of them if necessary! Generally, it is better to use the attack formation allowing optimal command and control to maneuver within striking distance of the enemy. At that time, the patrol may need to change attack formations to obtain the greatest security and make maximum use of the patrol's firepower.

The final consideration might be called "follow through." It is important not to exhaust the patrol to the point that they cannot continue the mission. Use the right formation for the given situation. That is the key to success.

CROSSING DANGER AREAS

I learned a long time ago the reason someone took the time to build a road, wear a path, or plow a field was because the terrain was pretty unforgiving. There was either too much vegetation, too much steep terrain, or both. So, one day, somebody with a lot of time on his hands built a road. Or, perhaps, they plowed a field to make farming easier. The point is that they created an easy means of maneuver—and a very dangerous place for soldiers to be.

The truth is that roads, paths, creeks, and open fields present fantastic opportunities for ambush and sniping missions. These natural and man-made obstacles allow for fairly long sectors of fire because they are relatively clear. For that same reason, they also entice lazy troops to patrol right through them. That's why these are "danger areas."

Danger areas fall into two categories—linear and open. Furthermore, each category has two subcategories—big and small. There are multiple methods in the bag of tricks to get safely across danger areas.

Why Use This Drill?

Crossing danger areas presents a series of battle drills that gets the patrol to the far side of the danger area with the very least amount of exposure and the maximum amount of necessary firepower positioned to deflect an enemy attack. Most commonly, this means maneuvering from one tree line to another, but it could also mean from one side of the city block to another, or even from one ravine to another. The point is to get through the danger area as safely and as quickly as possible.

Decision Points

First a PL must assess the type of danger area with which his patrol is presented. Ideally, the patrol circumvents a danger area—that is, goes around. However, linear danger areas rarely give that option. Instead, you must traverse these danger areas—that is, cross them.

The patch-to-the-road method uses speed as the primary form of security. A left and right security overwatch is provided locally only. Then, at the patrol leader's signal, the rest of the patrol charges in column file across the danger area. It is very fast!

So, a PL has to assess the type and relative size of the danger area. Also, the PL has to assess the likelihood of enemy contact. It's a pretty quick mental checklist:

- Linear or open danger area
- Big or small
- Significant or sparse enemy presence

What's all the fuss? Well, if moving through territory with significant enemy presence, hopefully leadership has allotted the patrol a realistic amount of time to conduct its mission. This means employing a more deliberate method of crossing the danger area—one that offers maximum amount of protection to the front and flanks. For a linear danger area, this might mean the **heart-shaped method**. For an open danger area, this might mean the **box method**.

On the other hand, if moving quickly through territory with sparse enemy presence, and time is of a high priority, cross the danger area with a method that makes maximum use of speed a form of security, with minimal protection to the front and flanks. For a linear danger area, this might mean the **patch-to-the road method**. For an open danger area, this might mean the **bypass method**.

Of course, the size of the danger area must also be considered. If the danger area is too large to use speed as a form of security, even in the case of patrolling through territory with a sparse enemy presence, it may be best to use a method offering a greater form of security.

Take Action!
Linear Danger Areas

The most common linear danger areas include roads or trails and the edges of creeks or rivers. However, they can be anything that channels a patrol's movement, such as fences, walls, or alleys. These obstacles provide the enemy with opportunity to ambush patrols.

Patch-to-the-Road Method

Using this method, a nine-man squad should be able to cross the danger area in ten seconds or less. *Speed is a form of security.* This method also allows the column formation to be maintained, which means greater control and communication for the PL.

1. The point man brings the patrol to a halt and signals that he has come upon a danger area. The PL comes forward to view the danger area, assess the situation, and select a method of negotiating the danger area.

2. If the patch-to-the-road method is selected, the PL communicates this to the team with the appropriate hand and arm signal. The entire patrol closes the intervals between members to shoulder-to-shoulder. The patrol members must actually touch each other. This is done even during daylight hours. This will allow a very fast pace when crossing and prevent a break in contact.

3. The two-man security team moves from the rear of the formation up to the front. At the PL's signal, the first security troop steps up to the danger area only as far as he needs to look left and right. If the road is clear of enemy presence, the troop takes a position so that he can view down the road to his right. In this position, his unit patch (on the upper part of his left arm sleeve) will be facing toward the middle of the road. Thus, the method is called "patch to the road."

4. As soon as the security troop on the near side of the danger area levels his weapon down the road, the second member of the security team immediately rushes across the danger area and takes up a position to view down the opposite direction of the road. At this point, both team members have their unit arm patches facing toward the middle of the road and they are pointing in *opposite directions.*

5. As soon as the security troop on the far side of the danger area levels his weapon down the road, the PL will stand up all of the remaining patrol members to RUN across the danger area. This is done literally by holding onto the gear of the troop to the front.

6. As the last troop passes the near-side security troop, he firmly says, "Last man." An acceptable alternative is to tap the security troop on the shoulder. In either case, this indicates to the security troop to stand up and run across the danger area behind the patrol.

7. The security troop will say firmly, "Last man," to the far-side security troop or tap him on the shoulder. This lets that troop know to follow behind.

8. Now, the entire patrol is back in its original marching order on the far side of the objective.

It is important that, as the point man initially crosses the danger area, he makes a quick dash into the tree line to visually inspect the space that the patrol will occupy. The *only reason to stop the patrol in the danger area* is if the point man determines the far-side tree line is booby-trapped. Even if the enemy has set up a near ambush, the patrol must assault through. No one stays in the danger area. Got it?

It takes considerable discipline and lots of rehearsals to keep troops facing down a linear danger area, partially exposing themselves and generally feeling vulnerable, when there is a hold-up, such as another member tripping while running

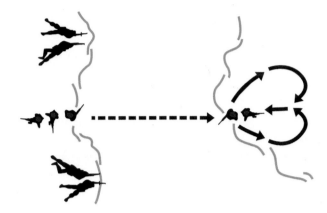

Crossing danger areas with the heart-shaped method makes maximum use of security and combat power. However, the heart-shaped method is time-consuming, making it impractical for small patrols who need to cross a small, linear danger area.

across the road, getting caught on a fence wire, or dropping an unsecured piece of equipment and doubling back to retrieve it. What generally happens at that point is one or both of the security team members become agitated and turn to look to see what's going on in middle of the road instead of maintaining a vigilant overwatch on their sectors. That's a real problem because invariably that's the moment when the enemy just happens to look down the road and begin shooting at the patrol!

Contingency Plan: Ideally, if the enemy does show up when your patrol is crossing a danger area, your security team will fire first! Or, if there is on-coming traffic, the security team will shout a warning to the other patrol to momentarily halt and hide. Obviously, this signal means no one else should attempt to cross the danger area. So, it is imperative that the security team realizes they are to keep a vigilant overwatch of the danger area until:

1. The patrol successfully traverses the danger area,
2. They are directed to hide from on-coming traffic, or
3. The patrol becomes engaged in a firefight.

What happens if there is a break in contact due to traffic or contact with the enemy? Each patrol must establish a method of re-establishing contact under just such a circumstance. Typically, if the patrol becomes separated, the patrol will rendezvous at the last designated en-route rally point (ERP).

The Heart-Shaped Method
If the patrol has to pass through a linear danger area in territory with significant enemy activity, or if the linear danger

area is simply too large to cross quickly with the patch-to-the-road method, then select a method with the greatest amount of security that the patrol can mass. This heart-shaped method takes about three to five minutes even for a squad-sized patrol. It also has a tendency to scramble the order of march and requires a great command and control. But, if rehearsed thoroughly, these issues can be mitigated.

1. The point man brings the patrol to a halt and signals he has come upon a danger area. The PL comes forward to view the danger area, assess the situation, and select a method of negotiating the danger area.

2. If the heart-shaped method is selected, the PL physically places a security team twenty to fifty meters down to the right and places another security team twenty to fifty meters down to the left. The exact distance depends on the terrain and visibility of the danger area. The PL returns to the main body of the patrol.

3. The PL now sends a third security team to the far side, across the danger area. The PL does not go with the far-side security team. Instead, the PL points out an easily recognized object on the far side that is in line with the patrol's direction of movement.

4. This team will cross the danger area as the situation dictates—perhaps at a run, perhaps at a crawl, or anything in between. They have immediate fire support from the left- and right-side security teams.

5. Once concealed within the far-side tree line, the security team conducts a quick listening halt to determine if the

Using the heart-shaped method, left and right security teams are placed on the near side of the danger area, and a security team is sent to the far side. Only after the "thumbs up" signal is given to indicate the far side is secure will the rest of the patrol cross.

enemy is in the immediate area. If enemy troops are detected, the security team carefully makes its way back to the patrol and informs the PL of the situation.

6. If no enemy is detected, the far-side security team physically inspects an area large enough for the entire patrol to fit. This is achieved by walking a designated distance into the tree line. Once they have walked that designated distance, the members turn away from each other and pace off a determined distance to check the flanks. The security members then move back toward their original listening halt positions. When looking at the path from a bird's eye perspective, it looks as though the security team has cut a heart-shaped path into the tree line.

7. When the security team has reassembled and determined the far-side security team is free from enemy presence, they give the PL the "thumbs up" hand and arm signal. This lets the PL know the far side is secure and that the far-side security team is monitoring the danger area.

8. At this point, the PL leads the remainder of the patrol, minus the left and right security teams, across the field using the same path as the far-side security team took earlier. The left and right security teams continue to monitor the danger area.

9. When the patrol is safely on the far side of the danger area, the PL will signal by hand or by radio for the left and right security teams to cross the danger area. They use the same path as everyone else.

Contingency Plan: If the patrol is compromised while crossing the danger area, the patrol will rendezvous back at the last ERP. However, the patrol cannot simply run away and leave its elements in the danger area. Without support, these troops will be killed or captured. Employ smoke canisters to screen withdrawing troops, and the left and right security teams place suppressive fire on the enemy until all patrol members have withdrawn. Once the patrol has withdrawn, the left and right security teams withdraw.

Open Danger Areas
Avoid open danger areas at all costs. This type of danger area covers just about anything not covered in the linear classification. Large open fields, small meadows, depressions, areas around large bodies of water, burnt-off areas, airstrips, and even parking lots are some examples of open danger areas. The good news is that these nasty obstacles are typically so large they show up on maps. Anticipate their presence, and plot a route around them. The bad news is that, sometimes, they're unavoidable, and those times force the patrol to go right through them.

The Bypass Method

The previously mentioned methods, patch-to-the-road and heart-shaped, are all fine and well. But, what if it is simply too dangerous to cross an open danger area? Enemy observation and fire can bring the mission to a quick end, especially if the patrol isn't supposed to make contact in the first place! In these cases, it's best to use the bypass. The bypass takes considerable time but offers the greatest degree of stealth.

1. After halting the patrol and signaling a danger area, the point man and the PL confirm the patrol's direction of advance using a prominent feature as a point of reference on the far side of the danger area. This may be an easily recognized terrain feature, such as a rise or dip in the terrain, or it

The bypass method is used for bypassing very large danger areas. The effort is for the patrol to fix on a prominent object on the far side of the danger area and then take several ninety-degree turns until it comes to the prominent object. Then, the patrol continues.

may be an easily recognized landmark, such as a tall tree or large boulder.

2. The PL estimates the distance to the far side of the danger area using visual techniques or the map. That distance is added that to their present pace count.

3. Then, ignoring the pace count and compass bearing, the patrol simply follows the point man as he skirts the danger area, keeping safely inside the tree line until the patrol gets to that designated feature on the far side of the danger area.

4. Here the point man assumes the previous direction of advance, and the patrol takes up the new pace count.

But what if the open danger area is so large that the patrol cannot even see the far side of it? One option is to deal with this terrain as "significantly thinning vegetation" instead of as a danger area, per se. In such cases, the patrol assumes a wedge formation and significantly increases the interval between patrol members and subordinate teams. The patrol continues to move along the direction of advance in this manner until the terrain changes. In other words, treat a very large open area in the same manner as an open desert or grass plain.

Crossing danger areas forces a series of battle drills that gets the patrol to the far side of the danger area with the very least amount of exposure and the maximum amount of necessary firepower positioned to deflect an enemy attack. There are two types of danger areas to be concerned with—the linear danger area and the open danger area. There are multiple methods for dealing with each situation, including the patch-to-the-road method, the heart-shaped method, the bypass method, and the box method.

The fact is that each danger area is a bit unique, and the PL will determine how to overcome each obstacle. The situation on the ground can change dramatically from what's on a map. For instance, a simple linear danger area on the map might actually turn out to be a massive open danger area once the patrol gets up close and personal with the terrain. In that case, the patch to the road method wouldn't be the wisest way to cross. Similarly, open danger areas on the map may actually be so overgrown that they present no danger area at all!

In addition to each danger area being unique, so are the requirements for different missions. A patrol engaged in a deliberate attack would handle a danger area very differently from a reconnaissance patrol. Even within a reconnaissance mission, a patrol on an area recon might be much more timid with danger areas than would a patrol on a zone recon. The important thing for a PL to do is to anticipate these danger areas, even if no danger areas show on the map. This is achieved through an established SOP for handling all types of danger areas and excellent rehearsals.

Finally, when faced with large open areas, consider the ranges of paintball and airsoft systems. Since most of these weapon systems have a practical range of 60 meters, larger areas present a real problem because the patrol can no longer fire in support of a far-side security team unless the left and right security teams are fitted with modified machine guns, designated marksman weapons, or crew-served weapons like mortars or rocket launchers. These systems can push the envelope out to 80, 100, and even 120 meters.

ESTABLISH A SECURITY HALT

Sometimes, a patrol has to stop and smell the roses, as they say. Regardless of the mission, every patrol must halt at different locations along the route. There are many reasons a patrol stops for a minute, or even an hour. The PL might need to confirm

When the patrol halts, take a knee. Standing upright may draw fire, and that won't make you very popular! Each troop faces in the opposite direction of the troop in front of him. The point man and drag man face forward and backward respectively.

his position on the map, the patrol periodically needs to listen and observe their new surroundings, or the patrol may just need a rest. This type of security halt is called the en-route rally point (ERP).

In addition to the ERP, every patrol makes a final stop prior to the assigned objective to coordinate between elements and make final preparations for actions on the objective. This type of security halt is called the objective rally point (ORP).

Why Use This Drill?

The ORP and ERP are security halts affording 360 degrees of security for the patrol as the patrol stops along its route toward the objective. Security halts provide concealment from enemy observation while plans and equipment are adjusted. The operative description for the security halt is *disciplined*. Noise and light discipline are strictly adhered to. This means no yelling or running from one end of the formation to the other!

The ERP is occupied, or at least designated, along the route. Ideally, it is designated at easily recognized terrain or landmarks offering cover and concealment. Again, the ERP does not need to be occupied, but it is still designated en route. Rarely is the ERP pre-designated in the plan.

The ORP is always pre-designated in the plan, placed far enough away from the enemy objective to conduct final preparations and planning before actions on the objective.

Decision Points

How close to the objective? It's hard to say. Stay safely concealed from enemy view and far enough away that the noise of final preparations won't be heard.

When halted longer than several minutes, take a step or two out in the direction you're facing and go to the prone position. Place rucksacks and gear to the front. This automatically forms a "cigar-shaped" perimeter with the command team center.

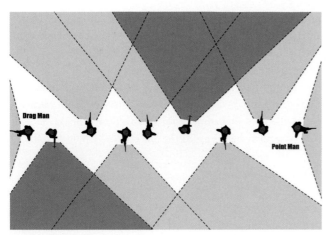

All troops should take a kneeling position upon a halt to lower their profiles. They continue to face in their primary directions for security purposes, affording 360-degree security. Troops continue to pass information up and down the formation.

The rule of thumb is to remain three hundred meters away, or one terrain feature. Keeping one sizable terrain feature between the ORP and the objective significantly reduces the chance the patrol will be detected. However, if the terrain is rather open, the ORP is kept at least three hundred meters away from the objective. In practice, this decision really depends more on the type of terrain, the size of the patrol, and the nature of the patrol's final preparations.

As for the ERP, the only consideration regarding when and where to stop would be concealment. Obviously, don't rally the troops in the middle of a road or open field. These are called "danger areas" for a reason!

Take Action!

Security halts are either taken by force or designated by a leader's recon that is sent forward to assess the anticipated site. The ERP is almost exclusively taken by force because there are so many unpredictable reasons for establishing an ERP. The drill most suitable for the ERP security halt is the "cigar-shaped" method.

The ORP, on the other hand, is a planned security halt and generally requires a leader's recon of the site to determine its suitability. In this case, the drill that is most suitable for the ORP is the "wagon-wheel" method.

Cigar-Shaped Method

A small patrol often walks directly up to the ERP or ORP security halt. This practice is known as occupying by force. The implications are that if the enemy is detected near the

security halt, the patrol either engages the enemy or quietly withdraws to a new position.

1. Upon reaching a desired location for the security halt, the PL halts the patrol. During halts, all troops automatically take a knee.
2. The PL indicates to the patrol members that they are in a security halt. Each patrol member faces either left or right in an alternating pattern and takes two steps outward to form a cigar-shaped perimeter. The point man, drag man, and PL are exempt from this maneuver and remain kneeling where they initially stopped. This leaves the PL in the center, the point man at twelve o'clock, and the drag man at the six o'clock position.
3. Subordinate leaders then ensure each man is behind adequate cover and assigned a sector of fire. At a minimum, the three, six, nine, and twelve o'clock positions must be maintained and covering their sector of fire.
4. The PL pulls any necessary leaders to the center in order to confirm or adjust plans. If this security halt is an ORP, the PL begins work priorities for the ORP.

Wagon-Wheel Method

Use this drill almost exclusively for occupying the ORP security halt. The effort is to get the entire patrol in a circular formation, and this takes considerably more work than the cigar-shaped

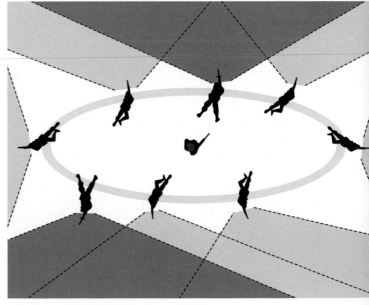

After a period of time designated by unit SOP—typically three minutes—the kneeling troops take a step forward in the direction they are facing. They look for cover, such as a thick tree or stone, and assume a prone position. This forms the "cigar-shape."

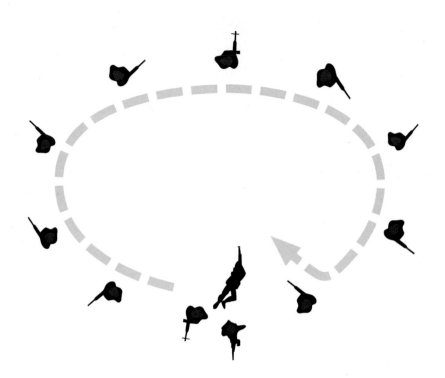

The wagon-wheel method of forming the ORP is one of the most simple. After a security team is placed as the anchor, the entire patrol plays "follow the leader" in a big circle. Once the circle is complete, the patrol leader adjusts the circle evenly.

method. Care must be taken in selecting the ORP site, as well as occupying it with the least amount of noise and commotion.

1. The patrol assumes an ERP security halt approximately one hundred meters from the planned ORP site. A leader's recon is then conducted forward at the ORP site to make certain the terrain is appropriate for use.
2. The leader's recon typically involves four members of the patrol—the PL, a compass man, and a two-man security team. Before leaving the ERP, the PL issues the assistant patrol leader (APL) a contingency plan and coordinates for their return.
3. Once the leader's recon has reached the designated ORP site, the PL determines if the site is appropriate or selects another site nearby.
4. The PL places the two-man security back-to-back at the six o'clock position of the ORP. Think of the security team as a couple of buddies saving a great parking spot. Don't leave the spot because someone else might take it. If a bad guy does takes the spot, you might find out he is much bigger and holds a black belt in karate!

    It's better to go back and say, "Hey, some really big scary looking guy just took our parking spot. Let's find another one." So, this security team will be left at the ORP to watch the spot and to guide the

remainder of the patrol into position. The PL will leave a contingency plan with the security team before the PL and the compass man return to pick up the rest of the patrol.

5. The PL and the point man return to the rest of the patrol back in the security halt. The patrol resumes its marching order, and since the compass man has already been to the ORP and back, he can lead the patrol right to the security team at the six o'clock position. The patrol halts once the compass man links up with the security team, and the PL moves forward.
6. From the six o'clock position, the PL leads the patrol in a large circular path around the perimeter of the ORP. This forms the patrol into a large circle through an exercise of "follow the leader."
7. Once the circle has been completed, the subordinate leaders adjust the exact positions of the members to offer the best cover and to provide 360 degrees of fire.
8. The PL pulls subordinate leaders to the center in order to confirm or adjust plans. The PL sets work priorities in motion for the ORP.

Work Priorities for the ORP

Once the ORP has been established, there is work to do. After all, the ORP is not the mission! The ORP is merely a

The wagon-wheel method is conducted by having the patrol leader simply walk in a circle around the area of the intended ORP. Troops are adjusted once the circle is complete. Typically machine gunners sit at twelve and six o'clock.

security halt where the patrol can finalize its preparations for the mission. Priorities of work are scheduled in the chronology listed below. Some of the work priorities are conducted concurrently. Some of the work priorities may not be necessary at all.

1. *Security is always the first priority!* The ORP never falls lower than fifty percent security. That means, whatever task is necessary, half the patrol maintains a vigilant guard of their sectors of fire.

2. *A leader's recon is conducted.* The leader's recon is optional and depends on the nature of the mission. The leader's recon team leaves and re-enters through the twelve o'clock position. It is coordinated with the patrol members in the ORP. Typically, the APL remains in the ORP while the PL, the security team leader, and a security team conduct the recon.

3. *All special equipment is prepared.* Don't prepare explosives, ready anti-armor weapons, or conduct radio checks while sitting in position on the objective! That is simply too much noise and activity, and the enemy will certainly see or hear the patrol. Instead, these preparations are conducted in the ORP, which is near the objective. So be quiet!

4. *Plans are finalized or altered.* The leader's recon may come back with surprising information that either slightly or dramatically alters the plan of the mission. Or, sometimes the failure of special equipment may require some improvising in order to complete the mission. In any case, these adjustments are made in the ORP, and every member must be informed!

5. *Weapons are prepared.* Weapons are cleaned if the patrol made contact while en route to the ORP, or if the movement to the ORP took considerable time and moved through a notably dirty environment—such as fording a river or being inserted onto a sandy beach. Still, no more than fifty percent of the patrol members do this at one time. The other fifty percent pulls security.

6. *Sleep and eating plans are initiated.* If the situation dictates, the ORP may implement an eating and sleeping schedule. Of course, fifty percent security is maintained, always.

Security halts offer 360-degree security when the patrol stops along its route toward the objective. Security halts

The triangle method requires a bit more coordination and is typically only used for larger patrols. Three elements make up three legs of the ORP—from two to six o'clock, from six to ten o'clock, and from ten to two o'clock, with machine gunners typically at each apex.

provide concealment from enemy observation while plans and equipment are adjusted.

The ERP is a security halt along the route. Ideally, it is quickly recognizable on the ground in case the patrol needs to return to it. The ERP is rarely pre-designated but is assigned or occupied along the route. When the ERP is occupied, it is almost always taken by force. The cigar-shaped method is well suited for this.

The ORP is the last stop prior to the objective, where the patrol can come together to coordinate with other friendly elements to finalize the mission plans and rest prior to actions on the objective. The ORP may be occupied by force—in which case the cigar-shaped method is used. More commonly, the ORP is first inspected by a leader's recon, and then the patrol is carefully maneuvered into position. In this case, the wagon-wheel method is used.

The ORP is dangerously close to the enemy objective! If the ORP is under limited visibility, the method of occupation is rehearsed prior to the patrol's movement. Noise and light discipline are paramount.

The method chosen to occupy a security halt depends on the terrain, the mission, and the number of troops available. But every combat mission will include security halts. Security is paramount.

ESTABLISH A PATROL BASE

A patrol base is not an end state but simply a position from which other patrolling missions conduct themselves. Obviously, selecting and establishing a patrol base is very important for sneaking into enemy territory and conducting further operations.

This chapter discusses a drill that establishes a patrol base. Remember, you may conduct this drill during daytime or nighttime conditions. It may be raining, snowing, or blistering heat, and this drill takes quite a bit of coordination. So, it must be rehearsed.

Why Use This Drill?

The patrol base is a temporary, forward, static position out of which a patrol conducts a series of missions. It offers cover and concealment from enemy observation. Security is maintained at 360 degrees inside the patrol base, and while there is no requirement to maintain a fifty percent security level at all times, the percentage of troops maintaining security is kept at a level the work priorities allow.

Remember, the goal is to go undetected. This means the patrol base is never used for more than twenty-four hours!

Decision Points

Where to place a patrol base? The rule of thumb is no closer than five hundred meters from the enemy force, or better yet, a major terrain feature away. To further conceal the position and the number of foot trails leading back to the patrol base, all subsequent patrols depart and re-enter the patrol base at the six o'clock position.

Build a defense? Again, the patrol base is a temporary position using concealment as its primary defense. As such, there is no need to develop fighting positions, bunkers, or trench systems. However, to provide a minimal amount of cover, some build-up of the patrol-base defenses should be tolerated as long as it's accomplished quietly! Entrenching tools and machetes make a good deal of noise. Barricades are preferable to digging, but hasty fighting positions or "shell scrapes" are permitted.

Take Action!

A variety of methods can help you establish a patrol base. Very small patrols might opt to take the patrol base by force, and the cigar-shaped method serves the purpose. Or, during daylight operations for small to mid-sized patrols, the wagon-wheel method suffices. Experience, however, has shown the "triangle" method affords the best use of crew-served weapons for defense and autonomy of subordinate teams.

Triangle Method

1. The patrol leader (PL) establishes an objective rally point (ORP) within 300 meters of the anticipated patrol-base site. The PL conducts a leader's recon of the patrol-base site, leaving a contingency plan with the assistant patrol leader (APL) back in the ORP. The

The triangle perimeter serves exceptionally well for patrol bases. It's formed using a four-step process. Step One: The patrol leader determines the direction of greatest threat as twelve o'clock and sets a security team at the six, ten, and two o'clock positions.

leader's recon includes the PL, the compass man, and a six-man security team.

2. Once the PL has inspected the site and is satisfied with the patrol-base site—or has chosen a suitable alternative—the PL leaves a two-man security team at the two, six, and ten o'clock positions of the patrol base with a contingency plan. Each security team is placed back to back. The PL and compass man move back to the ORP.

3. They rendezvous with the rest of the patrol in the ORP and inform them of any change of plan. The compass man is now familiar enough with the terrain to lead the patrol forward to the patrol base. If this is done at night, the security team member facing back toward the patrol must have a visual reference for the point man—a chemical light stick, flashlight, or illuminated compass lens. The compass man will link the security team with the rest of the patrol at the six o'clock position of the patrol base.

4. The PL then leads the first element from the six o'clock position up to the ten o'clock position. He then walks that first element from the ten o'clock to two o'clock positions and physically places each member of the element in a straight line between the two security teams. The PL then returns to the six o'clock position.

5. Waiting at six o'clock is the second element of the patrol. The PL walks the second element from the six o'clock to the ten o'clock positions and physically places each member of the element in a straight line between these two security teams. The PL returns again to the six o'clock position.

6. The third element waits at the six o'clock security team position. The PL links up with the third element and

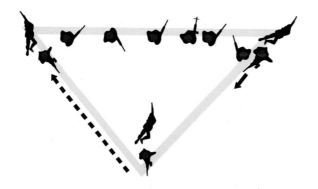

Step Two: The patrol leader walks the first fireteam or squad from six o'clock to ten o'clock and places them in a line from ten o'clock to two o'clock. These troops face the direction of the greatest threat— essentially twelve o'clock.

Step Three: The patrol leader returns to the six o'clock position to walk the second fireteam or squad in a line between the six o'clock and ten o'clock positions. The troop on the farthest left or right of each line must link up with the apex security team!

Step Four: The patrol leader meets the last squad or fireteam at the six o'clock position and walks them in a line between the six o'clock and two o'clock positions. Each apex is assigned a crew-served weapon, and the center serves as the command post.

walks them in a straight line between the six o'clock and the two o'clock position, physically placing each member of the element.

7. Last, the PL moves to the center of the patrol base to establish the command post (CP). The PL coordinates his subordinate leaders to be sure they are all aware of each other's location and tied into each other's left and right line.

Obviously, this complicated maneuvering takes a bit of practice. What is essential about this drill is that each security team must have two troops positioned back to back. This allows one troop to face out, providing security, while the second troop faces in the direction of the patrol to act as a guide. At night, the guiding member of each security team is required to have a light source that provides a visual reference for the approaching patrol members.

The triangle method is excellent for patrols with three elements—three fireteams, three squads, three platoons. A crew-served weapon is placed at each of the three apexes of the triangle—six, ten, and two o'clock. In this manner, no matter which direction the enemy approaches the patrol base, at least two crew-served weapons are brought to bear on the attacking force.

Priorities of Work

The patrol base is not a mission, per se. It is simply a means to an end, allowing the patrol to plan and conduct further missions. There is plenty of work to be done.

While the work priorities here are similar to the work priorities of the ORP, there are significant differences! Don't make the mistake of assuming everything is the same. What is spelled out below is the chronology of the work priority, though admittedly, some of these tasks will be achieved concurrently with other tasks, and some tasks will not be necessary at all. Which tasks are essential and which are not depends, of course, upon your mission.

1. *Security is always the first priority.* The patrol base is maintained at a level of security appropriate to the situation. As a rule of thumb, the patrol base does not fall below thirty-three percent security. That means one out of three troops are diligently watching their sectors of fire.

2. *An alternate defensive position is designated.* Typically, the PL informs the subordinate leaders that the ORP will serve as a fallback position in the event the patrol base is over-run. This information is disseminated to all of the patrol members.

3. *An ambush team covers the trail into the patrol base.* A small force backtracks approximately one hundred meters from the six o'clock position and steps off of the trail. This ambush team observes the trail for a half-hour or so to be certain no enemy force has followed into the patrol base. This must be done immediately after the patrol base has been secured.

4. *Communication is established between all key positions.* Field phones or radios are positioned with the CP and each apex at the two, six, and ten o'clock positions.

5. *An R&S team conducts a recon of the immediate area.* After communication is established, the PL dispatches a recon and security (R&S) team to skirt the area just outside the visible sectors of fire for the patrol base. Everyone must be informed! Otherwise, patrol members will fire on the R&S team.

6. *Mines and flares are implemented.* After the R&S team confirms the area immediately around the patrol base is secure, those positions designated to employ mines or flares carefully place them at the far end of their visible sectors of fire—no more than thirty-five meters out. These anti-personnel mines and early warning devices must be kept within viewable monitoring of the patrol base.

7. *Hasty fighting positions are constructed.* Barricades are the preferred method, as digging and cutting is too loud and may disclose the position. Fighting positions make use of available micro-terrain. If a hasty fighting position is necessary, care is taken to camouflage the exposed earth.

8. *Plans are finalized or altered.* The patrol's missions may be altered slightly or significantly in time. The PL makes these adjustments, and every member of the patrol base is informed. If at all possible, shoulder-to-shoulder rehearsals are carried out in the center of the patrol base, prior to conducting missions.

9. *Weapons are cleaned.* This is particularly true if the patrol made contact during a mission or if the movement to the patrol base took involved moving through a particularly filthy environment—such as fording a river or being inserted onto a sandy beach. Still, no less than thirty-three percent of the patrol members maintain security.

10. *Sleep and eating plans are initiated.* If the situation dictates, the patrol base implements an eating and sleeping schedule. Of course, security is maintained.

The triangle method is the most common for light infantry patrol bases. This is because, with a machine gun at each apex, an enemy approaching from any angle will be faced with at least one—and probably two—machine guns!

The patrol base is a temporary, forward, static position out of which a patrol conducts a series of missions. It offers cover and concealment from enemy observation and is never occupied for more than twenty-four hours.

Troops spend a disproportionate amount of time in patrol bases when operating in forward areas during maneuver warfare and within counterinsurgency warfare. Indeed, the patrol base is the only relatively secure position for patrols forward of the FEBA. As such, a concealed and secured implementation is essential. If the patrol base is at any time compromised, it is moved immediately. The patrol base is vulnerable to attack and is not intended to be a defensive perimeter.

The common mistakes patrols make when operating out of a patrol base include relaxing security and noise discipline, failing to conduct an initial ambush of the trail into the patrol base, and not implementing early warning devices like trip flares or anti-personnel mines. All of these infractions have a significant effect on the effort to keep the patrol base secure from attack. The results can be catastrophic. Good leadership and excellent discipline from the troops are the only solution.

ESTABLISH A HIDE POSITION

There are times when a small patrol operating forward of the forward edge of the FEBA needs rest. Perhaps the patrol entailed a march that could not be achieved in a single day or, more commonly, the patrol itself is of such a small size that a patrol base is neither feasible nor necessary. In these cases, the patrol can opt to implement a hide position to plan and rest.

Why Use This Drill?

The hide position is simply that—hiding. It is similar to the patrol base in that it is a security perimeter using concealment for its primary defense. However, the hide position is *not* a patrol base! It is only a place to rest.

There are several key differences between the hide position and the patrol base:

- No one departs or re-enters the hide position! No missions are run.
- It is used for no more than twelve hours and then is vacated.
- Hide positions are never re-used due to a risk of detection by the enemy.
- Fighting positions are not built up.

The hide position offers 360-degree security in that the entire patrol is positioned in a tight formation facing outward. Because the patrol is so close that they act as a single fighting position, as few as two men can easily maintain security. The hide position does not require any communication system other than word of mouth and bodily contact with the other troops.

Decision Points

Where to hide? Ideally, establish the hide position no closer than three hundred meters or a terrain feature away from an enemy force. Hide positions are intentionally placed in the most inhospitable terrain, such as in thick patches of thorn bushes or jagged rock formations. While a bit uncomfortable, this terrain discourages enemy patrols.

Take Action!

The PL designates the approximate location of the hide position on a map, or the PL may designate a condition under which the patrol establishes a hide position—such as after patrolling for a set number of hours or days. If the patrol is small, the PL may occupy the hide position by force. More often than not, this entails a bit of walking around in the desired location until the patrol locates terrain very difficult to traverse.

For a medium-sized patrol, the patrol establishes a security halt and sends a leader's recon forward to identify the hide position. At any rate, the PL indicates to the patrol that they are in hide position.

The "Back-to-Back" Method

This method is more practical for wooded and heavily vegetated terrain. When seated, the security team can observe the

When a hide position is placed in a heavily vegetated area without decent observation, the two troops pulling security will sit back-to-back to form a 360-degree security position. The remaining troops rest head-to-toe until it is their turn to pull guard.

likely avenues of approach or escape. This could not be achieved if the security team were lying in the prone in heavy vegetation. And frankly, if the patrol is exhausted enough that it has to use the hide position, placing the watch team on their bellies is just asking for trouble. An exhausted troop is much more likely to fall asleep lying down than sitting up—no matter how disciplined.

1. The patrol members come shoulder to shoulder, take a knee, and face left and right in an alternating pattern. All patrol members drop their rucksacks.

2. Designate half the patrol members to ready their sleeping bags and mats while the other half pull security. Once the first members have readied their sleeping positions as comfortably as possible, they sit on their equipment and pull security while the other members ready their sleeping bags and mats. No tents are pitched, no early warning devices are implemented, and no fighting positions are prepared.

3. The PL determines how many members of the patrol will pull security and what the duration and schedule of the guard shifts will be. Typically, hide positions require at least two troops to pull security at a time.

4. Since no anti-personnel mines or trip flares are used, CS canisters or fragmentation grenades are given to the first guard shift and passed to subsequent guards. If the enemy does walk nearby the patrol, great discipline must be enforced to allow the enemy to pass. On the other hand, in the unlikely case the enemy actually walks up onto the hide position, use grenades while the patrol makes a quick escape. Avoid direct fire at night since the muzzle flashes disclose the position and give the enemy an opportunity to suppress and destroy the patrol.

5. Radios are handled in a similar manner—passed from guard shift to guard shift—to keep in touch with higher command. If the hide position is occupied during nighttime hours, night-vision devices are also passed from guard shift to guard shift.

The "Star" Method

The star method is used for flat, open terrain, such as a desert, high mountain tundra, or grasslands. In this type of terrain, sitting up is less feasible because your position will be disclosed to enemy observation. So the entire patrol lies on the ground to lower their profiles.

1. The patrol comes shoulder to shoulder, and the PL instructs them to form into the star. The troops lie in the prone and interlock their ankles. This allows the security team to kick the man to their left and right to an alert status without making noise.

When the vegetation permits a decent field of observation, the troops lie prone to form a star. Two troops on opposite sides of the formation pull security while others sleep. They kick their buddies to alert status if a threat approaches.

2. Designate half the patrol members to ready their sleeping bags and mats while the other half pulls security. This responsibility changes hands while the other half of the patrol readies their sleeping bags and mats. Again, no tents are pitched because they are too easily visible, but rain tarps may be used to cover the patrol's sleeping bags.

3. The PL determines how many members of the patrol will pull security and what the duration and schedule of the guard shifts will be. Typically, hide positions require at least two troops to pull security at a time. Also, the two-man watch team will not be positioned right next to each other, but on opposite sides of the formation.

4. As you might have guessed, it might be a daunting task to find terrain that is difficult to traverse in the middle of the grassland prairie. The best a patrol could do would be to place a far distance between it and the enemy position and blend into the vastness of the countryside. Also, due to the ease of enemy movement in the open terrain, the PL may opt to use early warning devices or anti-personnel mines to slow an enemy attack.

Hide positions provide a reasonable amount of security for the rest of a small- or medium-sized patrol. However, when patrols become tired, undisciplined, or lazy, hidings are often overused due to the low requirement of security. Hidings have their purposes, but attempting to use a hide position as a replacement for the patrol base places the patrol in great danger. These two security positions have completely different functions, and the PL should never confuse the two!

If a larger patrol needs rest, the PL must establish a patrol base or a tactical assembly area and implement a sleep plan.

CHAPTER 4
ACTIONS ON CONTACT

HASTY ATTACK

This is it—the "Mother of All Battle Drills"—the hasty attack. The *hasty attack* drill is conducted when the patrol is in contact but *not engaged* by enemy fire. Compare that to the *react to contact* drill, which is conducted when the patrol is in contact and *engaged by fire*. Admittedly, these drills are remarkably similar in execution, but the hasty attack gives the patrol leader greater flexibility and time to form the patrol into an engagement benefiting the patrol. In short, the patrol can move more slowly and with greater stealth.

Before I go any further, maybe I should define the term "contact." Contact does not necessarily mean to be engaged in battle, although, it certainly includes that, too! However, visual contact is also a type of contact. The enemy may be completely unaware that you are observing him. *There is no need to blindly run into an engagement.*

The good news is that the hasty attack is a relatively simple battle drill. The bad news is that, if discovered, the enemy knows the drill, too! That's because, in essence, the effort is to overwhelm the enemy by flanking them. The flanking maneuver has been around since the days of the Greek phalanx.

Why Use this Drill?

So, what makes flanking such a successful method? The simple answer: Because a human can only fight in one direction at a time. Okay, that might be simplistic, but in practice it holds a great deal of truth. A more complicated answer might sound like this: A troop will pay attention to the nearest threat. An enemy with a knife that is five meters away is more dangerous than an enemy with a rifle fifty meters away, which, in turn, is more dangerous than an enemy with a mortar five hundred meters away.

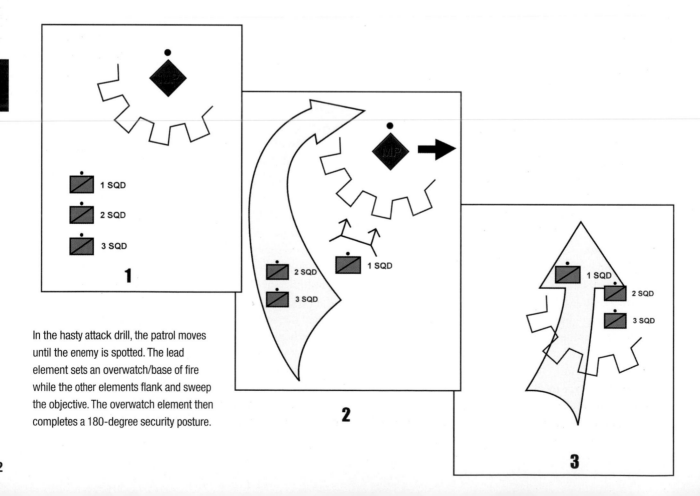

In the hasty attack drill, the patrol moves until the enemy is spotted. The lead element sets an overwatch/base of fire while the other elements flank and sweep the objective. The overwatch element then completes a 180-degree security posture.

As you get closer to your enemy, he will invariably attempt to put some cover between himself and you. Perhaps, he will hide behind a fat tree or stone. That's pretty smart. From this position, he will try to engage you as you move against his front.

However, as your buddy moves to his left or right flank, the enemy will generally pay attention to the closer of the two—or whomever poses the greater threat. When the enemy does this, he is opening up an opportunity for you or your buddy to defeat him. That is because a tree or rock only has so many sides! If he moves to avoid your buddy's assault, he will expose himself to your fire. It's pretty simple.

Of course a hole in the ground has many sides. But even in this case, the enemy's rifle can only fire effectively in one direction. So the same principals apply, which are:

1. Distract and suppress the enemy to allow your other team to maneuver
2. If the maneuvering team stalls, then they must distract the enemy
3. Your team now maneuvers against the enemy

The procedure is pretty straightforward and may be alternated between teams. The effort is to dislodge the enemy from their position, or better yet, completely destroy them.

Decision Points

Okay. Let's talk about decision-making. When your patrol makes contact with the enemy, you have three choices. You can **attack**, **defend**, or **withdraw**. And, that's pretty much it! Sure, the bypass moves around the enemy position, but that's just another form of withdraw. You might be tasked to fix the enemy, but again, that's just another form of defense. You're still going to sit tight and try to suppress the enemy so that another team can come crush them. Let's not get wrapped around the axle of the "intent." It all falls under attack, defend, or withdraw.

The leader of the forward-most team—most likely a fireteam, but possibly a squad or platoon—will have to make some quick decisions. The decision matrix is actually quite simple, when you stop to think about it. The decision-making process flows as illustrated in the diagram found in the next column.

That's pretty much it. To be certain, the decision to attack must follow the OPORD and ROE. Frankly, that most often means *asking someone for permission* to attack. Meaning that just because a fireteam leader thinks he can successfully attack

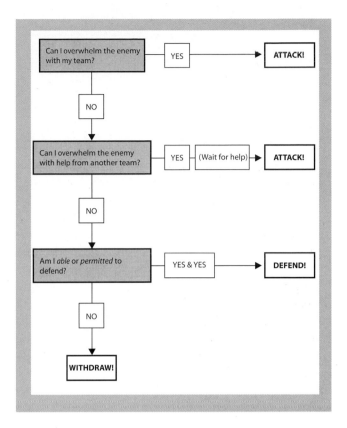

an enemy OP/LP, doesn't mean such an attack would benefit a platoon that is trying to achieve an element of surprise.

Another subtlety in the matrix is the decision to defend. There are two possible answers to the question, "Am I able or permitted to defend?" For example, your answer could be,

The hasty attack is a battle drill executed upon an enemy force that has not yet detected the patrol. Since the patrol is not yet detected, there is no sense in running until the shooting starts. Running before gives away the surprise.

yes, you are *able* to defend, but no, you are not *permitted* by your commander or the OPORD. If either of these answers is "no," then you must withdraw. If *both* of these answers are "yes," you must defend.

Take Action!

1. When the enemy is spotted, the PL is informed of the situation. If the PL decides that engaging the enemy is within the mission framework, the PL asks the leader of the element in contact—usually a fireteam—if the team can destroy the enemy alone. If the answer is yes, that fireteam attacks by fire and/or maneuver.

2. On the other hand, maybe the fireteam leader doesn't think he can handle the situation. If not, then the fireteam simply comes online, slowly and quietly. This fireteam now forms the base of fire. The trailing fireteam(s) begins to bound either to the left or right, using cover, to flank the enemy.

3. When the overwatch element engages the enemy, their fire is tenacious and accurate. This will draw the attention of the enemy immediately! It also masks the bound element's movement.

4. The bound team hits the enemy from an angle they are not prepared to defend. Shocked and losing troops as casualties, the bounding element suppresses and destroys the enemy, or the enemy will attempt to flee. At this time, the overwatch element **shifts fire**.

5. The bound element sweeps across the enemy objective and stops on the far side of the objective. The bound element leader signals the overwatch element leader to bring their troops forward. This forms the patrol into a 180-degree perimeter on the far side of the enemy objective. Now the patrol is prepared for a counterattack. The patrol leader and fireteam leaders reorganize and reconsolidate their patrol.

Note: Shifting or lifting fire has two positive effects. First, it ensures that the overwatch element does not shoot the bound element! That would be bad. Second, shifting your fire toward the escape route of the enemy, your patrol increases the likelihood of destroying the enemy as they escape. So—very important—shift fire away from the bound element and into the escaping enemy as the bounding element assaults across the enemy objective.

But, how far does the bound element actually move? The assumption is that the overwatch element is close enough to the enemy that they can place effective, suppressive fire upon the enemy if needed. If this is not the case, the overwatch element is almost useless. The patrol will have to move closer.

This means that a bounding element is already within a practical firing range of the enemy. So, at least theoretically, the bound team could maneuver the entire distance up to the flank of the enemy. Sometimes, the bounding element gets so close to the enemy that they take them completely by surprise. In these rare cases, the overwatch element doesn't need to fire a shot!

Note: *Don't be fooled by the term "bound."* It does not mean to run. Only run if everyone is shooting. If no one is shooting, *walk* quietly, and attempt to take the enemy by surprise. The term "hasty" only means the commander hasn't taken the time to issue an OPORD and rehearse.

Likewise, just because a team is providing "overwatch" does not mean it is shooting. Shooting at the enemy is called "suppression." Since, in this case, the enemy is *unaware* the patrol is observing them, the overwatch element simply continues to observe, ready in an instant to pour fire onto the enemy position if (1) the enemy discovers the bound team, or (2) the bound team signals the overwatch team to fire.

Though similar in execution, the discerning difference between the hasty attack and the react to contact drill is, in the case of the hasty attack, the enemy has not yet discovered the patrol. This gives your patrol enough time to carefully move into an advantageous position.

Upon contact, there are two key pieces of information the patrol leader and entire patrol will need to know. They include (1) the *direction* of the enemy and (2) the *distance* of the enemy. In the hasty attack, this information is disseminated quietly and quickly.

The hasty attack—like any offensive tactic—must seize the objective and provide a 180-degree security toward the retreating enemy force to guard against counterattack. At that time, subordinate leaders check each troop's water and ammunition and check for casualties.

In deciding whether or not to attack, the leader will proceed through a short series of questions:

1. Can I overwhelm the enemy with my team?
2. Can I overwhelm the enemy with help from another team?
3. Am I able or permitted to defend?

Assuming the attack is opted for, the lead element establishes an overwatch, and the trail element bounds to the left or right in an effort to flank the enemy position. Be aware that the bound and overwatch tasks *might* have to alternate between elements. This is particularly true for assaults across longer sections of terrain in which the patrol's longer-ranged weapon systems (crew-served weapons or modified marksman weapons/machine guns) may initially engage the enemy. In such a case, initiate fire well beyond the sixty-meter practical ranges of most paintball and airsoft systems.

As the bound element assaults onto and across the enemy objective, the overwatch element must shift its fire to avoid hitting its own troops, as well as to fire upon the enemy as they attempt to flee. The bound element stops and forms a defensive line on the far side of the enemy objective and then calls forward the overwatch element. The overwatch element moves forward to the far side of the enemy objective. They link up with the bound element and defend against a possible enemy counterattack in a 180-degree perimeter.

Finally, the patrol will reorganize and reconstitute according to LACE. Pay careful attention to key positions, such as subordinate leadership, crew-served weapons, and radio operators. From here, the patrol will call higher command to report the situation and ask for further guidance. In short, "Continue the mission!"

REACT TO CONTACT

During the hasty attack battle drill, the patrol has *not* been engaged by enemy fire. Seek the initiative and use stealth and mobility to surprise the enemy. That's the preferable course of action! But, what if the patrol *is* engaged by the enemy? In that case, use the react to contact battle drill.

The react to contact drill must follow the rules of engagement (ROE) established in the operation order (OPORD). However, once engaged by the enemy, the patrol doesn't have the time to request permission to return fire. Simply do it—immediately. The PL makes a quick decision to attack, defend, or withdraw and communicates this quickly to the entire patrol.

Why Use This Drill?

The react to contact drill seeks to destroy an enemy force through a chance meeting. While it's true that the patrol leader must quickly decide to attack, defend, or withdraw, each choice makes use of a different battle drill.

A decision to withdraw means the patrol utilizes the break contact drill. A decision to defend means the patrol forms online, seeks cover, and attacks by fire. A decision to attack means the patrol employs either the hasty attack or the react to contact drill. Obviously, if the enemy is shooting, the patrol *must* react to contact.

In order for the react to contact drill to succeed, it needs violence of action. A firefight involves a great deal of noise, and troops must yell over that noise. There will be communication through the entire drill, and this requires lots and lots of yelling. If the patrol is not making noise, they're not doing it right!

Decision Points

Most of the time, enemy fire is startling. It's not just being caught unprepared. Indeed, the engagement is anticipated in most cases. It's just that, if the patrol saw the enemy *first*, it would have taken an appropriate action that would have minimized the opportunity for the enemy to shoot.

So, most often, you must execute the react to contact drill under fire. It's an uncomfortable fact. This also impacts the decision-making matrix. In essence, the matrix still holds true, but the patrol leader comes to a conclusion *much faster* than with other drills.

React to contact is a battle drill executed when an enemy force that the patrol intends to destroy fires upon the patrol. The fireteam receiving fire lies prone and returns fire. The fireteam not receiving fire can then bound left or right to attack.

Furthermore, there will be no time to discuss these options with a higher command—not even if a higher-level leader is just another thirty, forty, or fifty meters behind. For this reason, the patrol leader abides by the ROE when deciding what action to take.

Take Action!

A keen observer might say, "Hey. Wait a minute. This is the same action as the hasty attack drill." That's factually correct. The effort is the same and the scheme of maneuver is the same for both drills. However, how the patrol communicates and how fast it moves are very different, since the patrol is now under fire.

1. When enemy contact is expected and the patrol starts taking incoming fire, all members of the patrol seek immediate cover. The fireteam leader closest to the enemy announces the direction and distance of the enemy: "Enemy! Ten o'clock at forty meters!"

2. Every member of the patrol repeats this, screaming at the top of their lungs. This ensures the patrol leader gets the message. *Speak! Be loud!*

3. The lead fireteam attempts to move online to suppress the enemy, as the PL goes through the decision matrix:

    A. Can the patrol overwhelm the enemy?
    B. Does the patrol need help?
    C. Can the patrol defend?

4. The PL makes the decision to attack, defend, or withdraw. Assuming an attack is preferred, and the fireteam in contact needs assistance (as is most common), the patrol employs the bounding overwatch technique.

5. The fireteam in contact continues to suppress the enemy. This fireteam becomes the overwatch position and employs a base of accurate, sustained fire. The noise and suppression also serve to mask the movement of other fireteam(s)—the bounding element.

6. The bound element moves left or right—whichever route provides the best cover. They come online with the enemy's flank and turn in to begin the assault.

7. The enemy pays attention to the greatest threat. If the enemy succeeds in stopping the advance of the bounding element, that is because the enemy has placed most or all of its fire at the bounding element. In that case, the bound halts their attack and comes online to assume an overwatch position.

8. The first overwatch position should be taking significantly less fire. They now become the bound team, moving toward the objective using a *different* route and attempting to assault across the objective. This process may change hands two or more times while the patrol is under fire.

9. Whichever fireteam assaults across the objective, the overwatching element will shift fire to avoid hitting friendly troops and fire upon the enemy fleeing from the objective.

10. The bound element sweeps across the enemy objective and stops on the far side of the objective. The bound element leader signals the overwatch position leader to bring troops forward. This forms the patrol into a 180-degree perimeter on the far side of the enemy objective. Now, the patrol is prepared for a counterattack from the enemy.

11. The PL and fireteam leaders reorganize and reconsolidate their patrol using liquid, ammunition, casualties, and equipment (LACE). These considerations ensure that the patrol has water and bullets, that casualties are being cared for, and that crew-served weapons and radios are being manned.

12. The PL reports the engagement and the patrol's status to higher command. Continue the mission.

The react to contact drill requires a great deal of violence of action. Bullets crack overhead and smack into nearby trees. The biggest mistake patrol members could make at this point would be to lose momentum—to sit down and not communicate.

Be aggressive. Use fire and maneuver. Always be conscious that part of the patrol will be *moving forward* against the enemy position at the exact same time as the other part of the patrol fires upon that same position! This is a dangerous dance.

The only way to perfect this orchestrated maneuver is to practice, practice, and practice. Remember, *perfect practice* makes perfect.

A word of caution: Remember, the enemy may engage the patrol with weapon systems that far out-range small arms. If the enemy engages at advanced ranges using crew-served weapons or modified systems—beyond the sixty-meter practical range of paintball and airsoft systems—the PL has the option of simply breaking contact. Obviously, charging headlong across fifty meters of open terrain just to come within small arms' range of an enemy position would risk needless casualties. If out-ranged, breaking contact is completely acceptable.

BREAK CONTACT

It is inevitable that, sometimes, the patrol must avoid an engagement. That's easy if the enemy hasn't yet detected and fired upon the patrol. If undetected, simply slip away.

If the patrol is already engaged in a firefight, breaking contact becomes a tricky situation. If the enemy's confidence is bolstered by the patrol's withdraw, the situation quickly becomes dangerous. Sensing a potential weakness, the enemy may very well charge forward with a great deal of violence and disregard for their own safety in hopes of delivering a fatal blow.

It is crucial that the patrol execute the break contact battle drill with precise fire and coordinated movements. Anything less than precision leaves the patrol vulnerable to enemy attack and potentially exposes the other members to friendly fire.

Why Use This Drill?

Break contact battle drills are used to escape further engagement with the enemy and evade continued pressure from a pursuing enemy.

Most of the time, when any two opposing teams meet, one team or the other has the advantage. This might be due to superior number of troops, superior use of terrain, or even superior weaponry. Whatever the case, if the patrol does *not* have the advantage, it's wise to break contact to avoid destruction.

Additionally, reconnaissance teams cannot effectively monitor the enemy and send reports to higher commands when decisively engaged with the enemy. Therefore, to break contact with the enemy is a common maneuver.

Decision Points

Using the decision-making matrix for enemy contact, you can see the option at the bottom of the chart says withdraw. Again, if the patrol is not engaged in battle, this maneuver is rather safe and simple. However, even when the patrol is engaged, the patrol leader may still come to the decision to withdraw. The break contact battle drill allows the patrol to do exactly that—while under fire.

Take Action!

1. The patrol leader announces the battle drill. He then designates which element will withdraw and a direction and distance for the patrol to withdraw. The entire patrol repeats this information by yelling loudly! It is essential that the patrol leader identify a specific fireteam or squad—by name—that will become the **displacing team**. It sounds very much like this:
   "Break contact! Bravo Team! Forty meters—Six o'clock!"
2. The displacing team might be the element closest to the enemy, or it may be the element furthest away from the enemy. The patrol leader makes this choice depending on

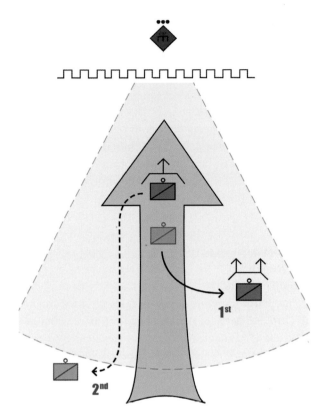

The break contact drill is used when the patrol comes in contact with a superior force. The lead team members attack by fire, and the patrol breaks contact while the trail team displaces to support by fire. The lead team then displaces, and the process repeats as the patrol falls back.

the specifics of the situation. That section of the patrol with the greatest survivability potential is typically the element to assume the role of the **suppressing team**.

3. In any case, the suppressing team increases the rate of their fire directed at the enemy—*regardless* of whether they can see enemy personnel or not. Under cover of this fire, the displacing team quickly moves in the direction and distance the patrol leader designates. They seek cover and immediately assume the role of suppressing team, placing a high rate of fire on the enemy position.
4. The forward-most element becomes the displacing team. They quickly retreat *past* the newly formed suppressing team, following loosely the same path. However, because this displacing team is still forward of the suppressing team, they must be very careful *not* to mask the suppressing team's fire! If the displacing team gets in between the suppressing team and the enemy, the suppressing team will stop firing, and the displacing team will be exposed to the enemy fire.

5. Once past the suppressing team, the displacing team seeks cover and immediately takes the enemy position under fire. This game of "reverse leap-frog" continues until the entire patrol is no longer taking effective enemy fire.

6. Then, the patrol sharply *changes direction of movement*. The patrol changes direction, taking a hard left or right turn in case the enemy decides to pursue the patrol. The patrol can continue a rapid withdrawal or may seek concealment to allow any pursuing enemy force to simply pass by them. The effort is to break contact and elude the enemy's effort to engage.

Employ break contact drills when necessary for the patrol to withdraw from an ongoing firefight. The patrol leader will initiate this option at the end of the decision-making process for actions on contact.

The patrol leader must communicate (1) the intended battle drill. He then designates (2) a direction of withdrawal, (3) a distance of movement, and (4) the element that will withdraw first—*by name!* Each member of the patrol repeats this information to ensure everyone has gotten the message.

The element that has been designated to withdraw is called the **displacing team**. The element that remains becomes, by default, the **suppressing team**. The suppressing team increases their rate of fire against enemy targets in order to cover the displacing team's withdrawal. The displacing team quickly runs in the designated direction and distance, takes cover, and assumes the role of suppressing team. Then, the former suppressing team becomes the displacing team and must run past the new suppressing team, being careful not to mask their fire.

This leapfrog progression continues until the patrol is no longer under fire, though the exact distance is more often dictated by terrain than by weapon systems. Realize the average paintball or airsoft system has a practical range of sixty meters. Once beyond this range and beyond the view of the enemy, the patrol changes direction to confuse any pursuing enemy.

Like all battle drills, rehearse until all patrol members understand their roles in the bigger picture and avoid friendly fire.

HASTY AMBUSH

The hasty ambush battle drill has many similarities to the hasty attack. In both cases, the patrol has spotted the enemy, and the enemy is not yet aware. The patrol has some time and space to maneuver, though stealth and surprise still play a large role in its success.

The principal difference between these two drills is that the hasty ambush is conducted on a *moving* enemy target, while the hasty attack is used when the enemy is more or less stationary. More specifically, if the enemy is moving in a given direction, and the patrol is able to maneuver into the enemy's path, it's an excellent opportunity to damage or destroy the enemy force using the hasty ambush drill.

Why Use This Drill?

The hasty ambush is not a tactic, per se. It's still a battle drill, which means there is little time for considerable assessment and a decision-making process. This battle drill allows the patrol to implement an ambush where they had not previously planned to do so.

Hasty ambushes may be conducted over long distances or very near the target. Caution: The patrol should only conduct the hasty ambush drill at close range if the patrol *outnumbers* the enemy—"close range" defined as within hand-grenade range.

Now, the patrol isn't required to assault across the objective, such as in a deliberate near ambush. In fact, this drill doesn't permit time for the patrol to break into specialized teams. More often than not, when the patrol conducts a hasty ambush drill, it will form online and simply conduct an attack by fire, using a high volume of fire and a great deal of violence of action.

Decision Points

The patrol leader uses the exact same decision-making matrix used in other battle drills. However, the middle option to wait for reinforcements is typically bypassed due to time constraints. After all, if the patrol waits any significant length of time, a moving enemy target will simply continue to move and leave the patrol far behind.

If the patrol leader believes the patrol can maneuver into the path of the enemy without being detected, *AND* the patrol is larger in numbers than the enemy OR can conduct the ambush at distances farther than hand-grenade range, he or she can implement the hasty ambush drill. Sometimes the enemy is moving directly at the patrol, however. In this case, the hasty ambush is more easily achieved without moving anywhere.

In the case of the hasty ambush, it is the decision to attack that prompts the ambush. The decision to withdraw simply means that the patrol could not feasibly maneuver along the enemy's path without being discovered. In this case, the best decision is to let the enemy patrol pass and then report the enemy patrol's size, activity, direction of

The hasty ambush is a battle drill executed upon a chance contact meeting with a moving enemy force that has not yet detected the patrol. It is very simply executed by lying on line and waiting for the enemy to enter the kill zone.

movement, and location to higher command. In this manner, another friendly unit might be able to set up an ambush and destroy the enemy patrol.

Take Action!

The first order of business is for someone in the patrol to detect and identify an enemy patrol. That troop immediately renders the "Enemy in Sight" hand and arm signal, which every troop repeats.

1. The PL moves along the patrol formation to gain the best vantage point to observe the enemy patrol. This may be done very slowly if the enemy is very close or if this occurs in open terrain.

2. The PL decides if the patrol has enough cover and concealment to move into position along the enemy's path. If the enemy is very near, the patrol leader only needs to decide whether the patrol is large enough to destroy the enemy force or if it should just let the larger enemy patrol pass.

3. Assuming the PL decides to conduct a hasty ambush, he gives the "Hasty Ambush" hand and arm signal. Immediately after, the PL gives the "On Line" hand and arm signal, indicating the orientation and location of the patrol's ambush.

4. Fireteams move their troops into position. They may have to do this relatively quickly or slowly. In either case, great care is taken to be quiet and to hide movement from the enemy patrol. In daytime, movement is quickly seen. At night, noise is quickly heard. In the most extreme cases,

the PL may indicate for everyone to stay still and NOT to move. This may be because the enemy is moving parallel to the patrol, which is already in position to fire. Or it may be because they simply cannot risk detection.

5. In the hasty ambush drill, the PL initiates fire and the entire patrol joins in like one long firing squad. *Everyone shoots!* The effort is to absolutely stun and destroy the enemy patrol with an attack by fire.

6. The PL determines if the enemy has been effectively destroyed. If the enemy offers little resistance, the PL yells "cease fire!" He may choose to sweep the objective by keeping the entire patrol online and moving aggressively against any remaining enemy. Alternatively, if the enemy is still putting up a fight, the PL may choose to fall back to the last en-route rally point (ERP) using the break contact battle drill.

7. If the patrol sweeps the objective, fireteam leaders keep the troops online and move just over the kill zone to the far side of the objective. Patrol members may be called out by name to search for priority intelligence requirements (PIR). Fireteam leaders reconsolidate and reorganize the patrol using the considerations of liquid, ammo, casualties, equipment (LACE) and prepare to move out. They must move out of this engagement area quickly or risk counterattack.

8. If the patrol breaks contact and falls back to the last ERP, the PL forms the patrol into a 360-degree security, reconsolidates, and reorganizes, using the considerations of LACE. The PL reports the engagement and patrol status to higher command. Continue the mission.

The hasty ambush drill allows the patrol the opportunity to ambush a moving enemy patrol, even though it hasn't deliberately planned or prepared for an ambush. This is a situational opportunity in which the patrol maneuvers into the path of the enemy and destroys the enemy using an attack by fire.

A very high volume of fire and violence of action is thrust at the enemy force to stun them and keep them from making an effective counterattack. But, in order to achieve this effect, the patrol must first detect the enemy and maneuver stealthily into position. If the enemy sees or hears the patrol doing this, they will simply change directions and bypass, or worse, they may attack.

React to Ambush

There exists a plethora of ambush types and variations—area ambush vs. point ambush, hasty ambush vs. deliberate ambush, plus the numerous methods of ambush. Confused? There's no need to be. The many different considerations of the ambush only apply when the patrol is *conducting* the ambush. When *reacting* to an ambush—that is, when the patrol is the target—there are really only two types of ambushes with which to be concerned—the **near ambush** and the **far ambush**.

Now, be aware there has been an ongoing debate for years among tacticians regarding the react to ambush battle drill. The disagreement centers on whether a patrol should react to an ambush by assaulting immediately through the enemy lines or by seeking cover and assaulting by fire. The answer is *both*.

What this means is, like many other battle drills, there should be more than one version of the drill in a patrol's arsenal of options. In fact, there should probably be half a dozen different variations for the patrol's reaction to ambush at a minimum!

Why Use This Drill?

Regardless of whether or not the patrol has stepped into a near ambush or far ambush, getting out of the kill zone is the highest priority! The kill zone is deadly. That is where the enemy has anticipated and prepared for the patrol's arrival. If they've done their job well, everything about the kill zone is bad for the patrol and good for the enemy. So, get out of this mess quickly.

For a near ambush, the patrol must move *through the enemy's line*. This will greatly upset the enemy's carefully laid plans because their target is moving out of the kill zone. Furthermore, the target is moving *into* and among the enemy's own troops! This makes it much more difficult for the enemy to engage the patrol without placing their own troops in danger of fratricide.

For a far ambush, the patrol must *get out of the kill zone the same way they came in*. The far ambush has less dominance over the kill zone than the near ambush. This means that any part of the patrol that is in the kill zone should seek immediate cover. Then, all members of the patrol must return fire and use smoke to mask its withdrawal. Once out of the kill zone, the patrol has the option of counterattacking the enemy ambush or simply bypassing it.

Decision Points

When a member of the patrol detects an enemy ambush, this information must be communicated. The patrol leader has two urgent questions to answer:
1. Is the patrol in the kill zone or under fire yet?
2. How close is the enemy ambush? (Giving consideration to terrain.)

Being in a far ambush—while very dangerous—is not as bad as being in a near ambush kill zone. The best way out is the way you came in! Troops caught in the kill zone lie down and return fire. Use smoke to mask withdrawal of any troops in the kill zone. Then, counterattack.

Is the Patrol in the Kill Zone?

Fully half of all ambushes are seen or heard by the targeted patrol *before* the patrol enters the kill zone. In these cases, the patrol leader must be informed of the impending ambush. The patrol leader then assesses the situation and quickly selects the course of action for the patrol. At this point the patrol will *not* execute the react to ambush battle drill!

Why? Because the patrol is not in the kill zone yet. Only execute the react to ambush drill if part or all of the patrol is *in the kill zone*. If the enemy ambush is discovered, the patrol may opt to conduct a hasty attack or simply sneak away and bypass the enemy.

So, the choice of battle drill depends first on whether the patrol has discovered the enemy ambush before the patrol enters the kill zone. If you aren't certain, take a guess. But, generally, if the enemy isn't looking in the direction of the patrol, chances are good the patrol is outside the kill zone.

How Close Is the Enemy?

Is the enemy near or far? For the sake of this discussion, it may help to picture "near ambush" in terms of hand grenades. The average man can throw a hand grenade approximately thirty-five meters. So, *within* hand-grenade range is determined to be "near." Significantly farther than thirty-five meters is determined to be "far."

If the patrol finds itself in the regrettable position of being in the enemy's near ambush kill zone, there is only one way out—through the enemy! Do not lie down, but attack immediately and aggressively. Violence of action is the only hope!

But wait a minute. In the jungle, hand-grenade range is much shorter. This is because tree limbs, vines, and heavy vegetation slow down the grenade. A troop must throw with a great deal of care or the grenade will bounce back! "So what?" you say. Well, if a tiny little grenade cannot easily get through the heavy vegetation of the jungle, then neither can *you*. Ultimately, the rushing distance determines a near ambush from a far ambush.

So, if the patrol can quickly rush into the enemy line, it is a near ambush. If not, it is a far ambush. In heavy vegetation, the patrol would be hard pressed to rush fifteen meters! In flat, open terrain, a grenade will travel much further, and so will the troops. A near ambush can be as far away as fifty meters. The thirty-five-meter range is just a rule of thumb and works well for most environments, but not all. Anything beyond hand-grenade range should be considered a far ambush.

Let me say it this way: if you're in a kill zone and can quickly get into the enemy's line, then you should. If you're not close enough to rush in quickly, then don't! Your team will be unnecessarily laid to waste in front of the enemy machine gunners. Seek cover.

Take Action!
Near Ambush
The near ambush is described as a surprise attack from a concealed position upon a moving or momentarily halted target that is *within rushing distance*. Keep in mind that sniper fire received within rushing distance would also be considered a near ambush.

When properly executed, an enemy ambush team will fire into their kill zone for only as much time as it takes them to effectively engage their targets. Depending on the size of the ambush team, this takes perhaps fifteen to thirty seconds. Afterward, the enemy will either begin movement into their escape routes, or they will send forward a team to assault the survivors left in the kill zone. That's not a very pleasant thought.

If the patrol members seek cover in the kill zone, fumble through their gear to find a hand grenade, wait for those grenades to explode, and then attempt to coordinate an attack by fire, their time to react is squandered. The enemy has either already begun their escape, or the enemy assault team will soon attack while the patrol is still in a state of panic and disarray. Either way, that's not good.

Furthermore, you'll become isolated if you lie down. You won't be able to see your teammates or communicate with them. You won't attempt to gain the initiative because you'd have to go it alone. If you're lucky enough to survive the initial volley of fire unscathed, guess what comes after those first fifteen seconds? That's right—the assault team! There is no choice when you stop to think about it. You have to move through the enemy's positions, and you have to do this immediately.

The enemy ambush team is in a static position. They have carefully planned their sectors of fire so they will not shoot each other. Now, this may seem so obvious that it is something of an overstatement. On the contrary, that can work in your favor. So, for the moment, remember that the enemy does not want to shoot members of their own patrol.

Your patrol, on the other hand, is in a dynamic position as you move into the kill zone. Moving targets prove to be difficult to kill because they readily pass from one sector of fire to the next. If this sounds a bit trivial, consider that a well-executed near ambush has only about fifteen seconds to coordinate its initial volley of fire. It's awfully hard to hit multiple, moving targets under such time restraints.

Wait. If each member of the enemy ambush team is assigned a sector of fire, what does he do if a target inside the kill zone moves *out* of his assigned sector of fire? The answer to this perplexing question is that the member of the ambush team will either:

- Continue to fire only at targets inside his sector of fire and ignore all other targets
- Stop firing because there are no targets in his sector of fire
- Disregard his sector of fire and fire upon the target even after it leaves his sector

None of these options are very desirable for the enemy, and frankly, the most commonly selected option is the last—which is also the worst case for the enemy ambush team!

If the enemy continues to fire upon you while you rush into their line, that means they are placing deadly suppressive fire against members of their own team as well! As you may imagine, this is not conducive to morale or tactical performance. If they do not fire upon you as you leave their kill zone, you are free to fire upon them. It's a lose-lose situation for the enemy.

On the other hand, if you try to run away from the ambushing team, your back is turned to them. As you move away from the kill zone, you enter the beaten zone, which is even deadlier. Furthermore, a well-planned ambush will utilize natural or man-made obstacles to slow your escape when you enter the beaten zone. These obstacles will either expose you to enemy fire or simply employ land mines to end your escape. Not a pretty picture, no matter how you look at it. So, go through the enemy line.

The Best Way Out of a Near Ambush

1. At the very moment any member of the patrol determines his patrol is in an ambush kill zone, he screams at the top of his lungs the name of the battle drill and a direction (left, right, or forward). For example:

   "Near ambush—left!"

Too often, this moment is only realized just after the initial shot is fired from the ambush team, but no matter. The drill is still the same.

2. Every member of the patrol turns and rushes in the direction called out or simply toward the nearest amount of noise if they did not hear the direction—without hesitation! Do not lie down. Do not ask questions. Do not fumble around with hand grenades. If you try to do any of these things, you will remain inside the kill zone, you will isolate yourself from your patrol, and you will soon be killed!

3. Upon entering the enemy line, all members fire left and right to disrupt and kill the enemy. This forces the enemy ambush team to either fall back or be destroyed.

4. Only now can the patrol leader take cover and communicate with patrol members. Members of the patrol who are NOT in the kill zone must flank to engage the enemy line.

The effort here is, first, to get you out of the kill zone and, second, to break the enemy line. The ambush is a tenacious and volatile place to be. Only with extreme violence can your patrol disrupt and repel the enemy ambush team. Being inside the kill zone is regrettable, and you should expect to have casualties, but that does not mean the patrol cannot survive an ambush. The patrol must use the enemy's need for organization against them and react violently and immediately.

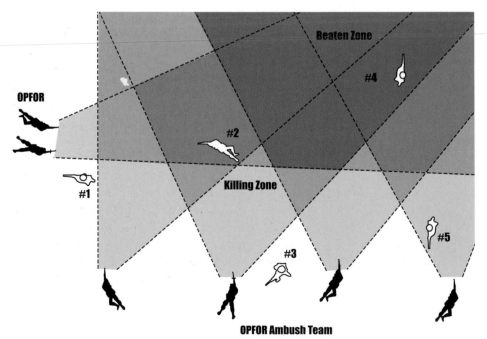

WRONG: Troop #2 has lain prone and become isolated. Troop #4 is running into the beaten zone. CORRECT: Troops #1, #3, and #5 are properly exercising the drill—rushing immediately through the enemy's ambush formation as quickly as possible!

Beaten Zone

OPFOR

#4

#2

#1

Killing Zone

#3

#5

OPFOR Ambush Team

Far Ambush

The far ambush is a surprise attack from a concealed position upon a moving or momentarily halted target from a distance *too far to be rushed across*. Sniper missions are typically conducted at far distances and are considered far ambushes.

In the far ambush, the enemy wants to keep a safe distance from the patrol, probably because it outnumbers them. The far ambush is conducted at greater distances in order to:

- Allow a small ambush team to fire upon a larger patrol or convoy;
- Avoid the risk of detection that is inherent in near ambushes; and
- Allow enough time and distance to escape if the targeted patrol moves to attack.

Often the targeted patrol is not entirely positioned within the kill zone. Those patrol members who are taking fire inside the kill zone must seek immediate cover! The first priority is to get the exposed troops safely out of the kill zone, then have the option of counterattacking the enemy ambush. If the patrol maneuvers quickly and decisively, it will be able to engage the enemy as they withdraw and turn the tables on them. But, the patrol must coordinate quickly.

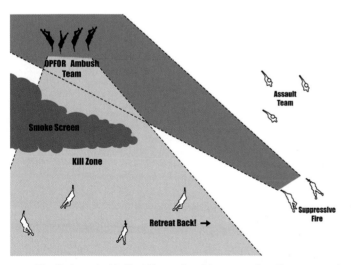

The fireteam inside the kill zone has taken cover, has thrown a smoke canister to conceal their movement, and is withdrawing out of the kill zone the same way they came in. The fireteam outside of the kill zone is properly counterattacking from the enemy's flank.

The Best Way Out of a Far Ambush

The enemy ambush patrol is rarely seen in a far ambush. Unfortunately, this means that the first indication that the patrol has entered a far ambush is being shot at.

1. At the sound of the first shot, all members of the patrol should fall to the ground and get a fix on the enemy's position.
2. Everyone then shouts "far ambush" and the enemy's direction and distance using the clock method. For example:
"Far ambush! Three o'clock—one hundred meters!"
3. All patrol members will employ suppressive fire until those troops in the kill zone have escaped. Employ smoke canisters to screen withdrawal from the kill zone, and escaping troops seek a low, defiladed route such as a ravine. Sometimes, troops simply run out of the kill zone. Hey, if it works, it ain't stupid.
4. The patrol leader then communicates the next course of action. The patrol will either attack by fire, attack by bounding overwatch, move around the flanks and seek the enemy in their escape routes, or simply bypass the enemy.

The kill zone of an ambush is a very dangerous place to be. The first order of business is to get out of the kill zone—quickly! In a near ambush, the entire patrol rushes through the enemy line. In a far ambush, use covering fire and concealment to escape the kill zone from the same direction the patrol came into it.

The near ambush is a very personal fight at incredibly close ranges. The far ambush, however, allows the PL to make better use of the patrol's crew-served weapons and/or designated marksman weapons. Because these modified paintball and airsoft weapons achieve practical firing ranges of up to one hundred meters and beyond, these weapon systems will be key in suppressing enemy fire.

Minimize casualties by rehearsing slight variations of these two battle drills. It's best to have multiple options in the bag of tricks. Rehearsals also increase effectiveness in defeating an enemy ambush.

Perhaps the main learning point is this: the enemy is not stupid. If you plan to establish just one drill for all possible scenarios, the enemy will respond by countering your single drill with the course of action that best suits him. Be flexible. Have more than one solution and rehearse them all!

SECTION 3
TEAM TACTICS

Because defense is the stronger position, defend long enough to mass and plan, but remember the offense is the only means of imposing will upon enemies. This means the offense is the preferred position. Tactical victories lead to operational victories which, in turn, lead to strategic success. Work the problem at hand, but keep one eye on the future. As the battlespace changes, be prepared to exploit the enemy's weakness and achieve victory.

CHAPTER 5
PATROLLING PRIMER

PATROLLING OVERVIEW

Teaching patrolling over the years, I've come to view each lesson as a single piece of a large jigsaw puzzle. Many tacticians see the pieces but not the whole picture. That's problematic. If you cannot see the big picture, how do you know where and when to use each piece? Yeah. Patrolling can seem quite intimidating—particularly for a small unit leader tasked with *planning* a patrol.

The good news is that patrolling concepts are not new to you. You've used them all your life on a daily basis, though you never realized it. So what I like to do is to tell a story that is common to human experience in order to illustrate all of the phases of a patrol.

Planning Phase: Troop Leading Procedures

Let's start with an earlier experience in life, common to all—back in high school. Let's say your older cousin lets you in on a little secret, telling you that there will be a party Saturday night at his buddy's home in the next town. Guess what? You've just **"received the mission."**

And what do you do? Right away, you get on the telephone and call up several of your closest friends! You tell them the date, time, and place of the party, and you tell them to meet you in your garage Saturday to finalize the plan. And that's it. What you've just done is **"issued a warning order"** (WARNO).

A warning order consists of the mission (the party) and the time and place it is expected to begin. Most importantly, the warning order will include the time and place of the operations order (in your garage), where you will finalize your plan. And you gave them all of that!

Now, all you have to do is coordinate who will drive, a road map to where you are going, places to stop and get gas, and how to get some cash. You'll also make a plan of when and where to meet after the party so that everybody gets home and no one gets caught in this plan of deception. And ta-da! You've just **"made a tentative plan"** and **"conducted a reconnaissance,"** since you looked at a map to find directions to the party. On Saturday night, as your buddies leave their homes to come over to meet you in the garage, that's known as **"starting movement."**

The squad is the essential fire and maneuver element. It is the building block of all infantry units. The squad may break into two or three fireteams made up of riflemen, automatic riflemen, machine gunners, grenadiers, and rocket launchers.

Of course, you don't think of going to a party in these terms, but I assure you, you've planned and executed many patrols in your life. You will have to **"complete the plan."** Some patrols are as simple as going shopping, meeting family for religious worship services, or going on vacation. So, you're sneaking out of your parents' home to go to a party on Saturday night—that *is* a patrol.

In the garage of your parents' house, you meet your buddies and quickly discuss the plan, the route, and everyone's responsibilities. That's it. You've just **"issued the operations order"** (OPORD). You may go so far as to **"rehearse"** your excuses if a parent or close friend of the family catches you drinking or rehearse your charming manner of collecting phone numbers for a future date.

Finally, since you put together the plan and therefore are the default leader, you will have to continually **"supervise the process"** throughout the night to make sure everything is going according to plan. For example, *do not* allow your designated driver to drink! If a cop stops you while driving home, the entire plan just became a nightmare! And, your parents will have to come to the police station to get you. Bad. Very bad. (Trust me, I speak from experience here.)

That's all there is to troop leading procedures for the patrol. You see? These are things that you do *naturally*. There is nothing new here. Don't let it overwhelm you. It's very much the same process whether your patrol is going to a party or on an attack.

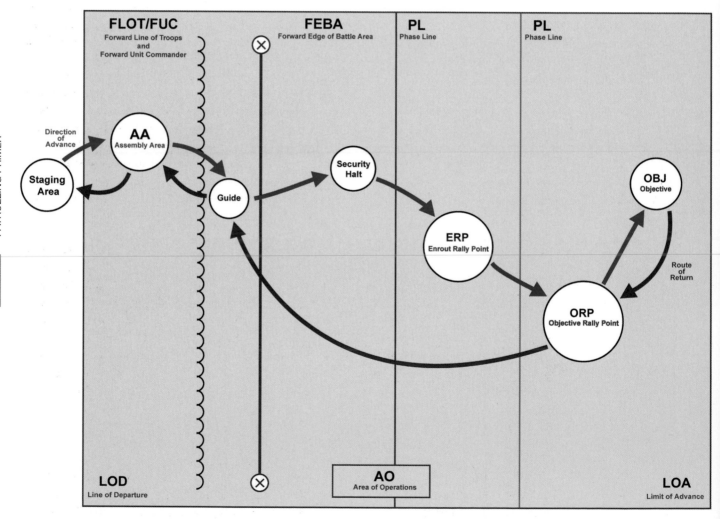

Patrols start in a staging area and cross the line of departure (LOD) into the forward edge of battle area (FEBA). At the assembly area (AA), a passage lane is coordinated through the forward line of troops (FLOT) with a guide, and the patrol conducts a listening halt once past the FLOT. Movement is reported via phase lines (PL). Plans are finalized in the objective rally point (ORP) just prior to the objective (OBJ).

Action Phase: Patrolling

The physical spot where you meet with your buddies in your garage is called an **"assembly area"** (AA) which is within the part of the battlespace known as **"forward edge of battle area"** (FEBA). The AA is where you develop your plan, rehearse, and conduct a **"passage of lines."** But, you still have to coordinate with your dad—the **"forward unit commander"** (FUC)—for the use of the car and for the time you must return. Don't forget to coordinate with your mom for some cash—the **"supporting unit commander"** (SUC).

Your know-it-all younger sister will act as your **"guide."** The way to keep her happy and quiet about your plan is to promise to pay her if she washes the car tomorrow after you return. You will throw a small twig at her bedroom window tonight when you get home. Your sister will quietly open the garage door to let you in so you can get some sleep in your own bed. This is known as **"coordinating the departure and return signal"** with the guide.

Now, your patrol is operating alone. You have left your family—the **"forward line of troops"** (FLOT) and are passing through the neighborhood.

When you get out of town, you will have to stop and fill up your gas tank. This stop is known as the **"security/ listening halt."** Here you stop to orient yourself to the map and terrain and to listen to hazards like police sirens or your mom calling your cell phone! Your buddies run inside to make themselves comfortable for the trip, grab snacks, and fill up on gasoline. After a few minutes, you start moving toward your **"objective"** (OBJ)—the party.

On the drive to the next town, you see a well-lighted motel. You tell all your buddies, "If we get separated tonight, everyone should try to make it back to the parking lot of this motel. We'll wait for you here." That makes perfectly good sense. And, in military terms, that is known as establishing an **"en-route rally point"** (ERP).

You drive into the next town. Because you've looked at your map, you know that you will soon come to the house where the party is. You drive up to a long line of parked cars and hide your car among the others. After all, you don't want friends of your parents to recognize your dad's car!

Since you will all be returning to the car after the party, this parking lot is called the **"objective rally point"** (ORP). However, if you did not plan to return to the parking lot—perhaps because you all expected to hook up with a date for the evening—then the parking lot would be called an **"assault position."** That is a fine distinction. If we *will return*, it's called an Objective Rally Point. If we *will not return*, it's called an Assault Position.

In either case, it is the last place to stop before moving onto the objective. It is also the last opportunity to adjust your plan—but only if absolutely necessary. Beware: a new plan might confuse your friends.

The front door of the party house is called the **"release point."** This is where you, as the commander, release authority to all of your subordinate commanders (a.k.a. "your friends"). In short, it's everyone for themselves!

Every mission has its specific **"actions on the objective,"** which detail exactly how success will be achieved. In the case of the party, your goal is to drink, dance, and flirt incessantly with the object of your desire! But, you get the point.

Because every mission has its dangers, you must always assign an **"aid and litter team"** to carry the wounded. This is particularly true if there will be excessive drinking. Additionally, you will have to **"designate a withdraw"** time, or signal, or condition. This will tell everyone on your team when to leave, and they will leave through the Release Point—the front door, remember?

Once back in the parking lot, you conduct a **"head count"** as everyone gets into the car to make sure you've left no one behind. Now, you can begin to tell stories about how many phone numbers you were given and who kissed whom. These stories are **"disseminating information."** And it is very important to remember these stories and share with everyone once back home.

At this point in the mission, your team just needs to fall back and regroup. You'll probably go to a late-night restaurant to get some coffee and food. You'll need to sober up a little before going home. This stop is called a **"security halt."** If you're really smart, you'll call your younger sister on her cell phone to tell her you will be home soon. That way she will be awake when you arrive. In military terms, this is called the **"far recognition signal."** It is given well before the Guide (your sister) sees you.

You drive back to your hometown and to your house. Your car is waiting outside the garage, and you throw a small twig or pebble at your sister's bedroom window. This is called the **"near recognition signal,"** since she can look out the window and physically recognize you.

When your sister opens the garage door, you and your buddies **"reenter the friendly forward line"** (FFL)—the garage door. You **"count everyone by name"** for your sister. This allows your sister to be sure (1) that everyone made it back and (2) that no strangers are being allowed into mom and dad's house!

Quickly, you talk to your buddies, now that you have **"reoccupied the assembly area"** (AA)—in the garage. You

Each patrol will face any number of possible situations, and there must be a contingency plan for each possible situation. That is why it is essential to learn the sequence of events each patrol necessarily entails.

must coordinate your stories and share your stories only on a **"need-to-know basis."** That will anger your sister, but she'll be okay in the morning when you pay her cash.

That's it. You've completed an entire patrol. And, you do this on a regular basis! Don't let the military terminology intimidate you. Sure, sure, it's important for you to understand the language. That way, all elements can communicate. But the *concepts* are the same thing you've been doing for years.

Planning Phase:
1. Receive the mission
2. Issue a WARNO
3. Make a tentative plan
4. Conduct a reconnaissance
5. Start movement
6. Complete the plan
7. Issue an OPORD
8. Rehearse
9. Supervise the process

Action Phase:
1. Occupy the AA
2. Coordinate passage of lines with the FUC and SUC
3. Coordinate departure and reentry of the FFL with the guide
4. Guide through the FLOT—pass through the FEBA
5. Establish a security/listening halt

6. Move along route toward OBJ
7. Designate (at least one) ERP
8. Occupy the ORP or assault position
9. Enter OBJ through the release point
10. Conduct actions on the OBJ (. . . this *is* the mission!)
11. Exit OBJ through the release point
12. Reoccupy ORP and take a head count/disseminate info
13. Move along route toward FFL
14. Establish a security halt
15. Issue far recognition signal
16. Issue near recognition signal
17. Reenter FFL
18. Count team by name
19. Reoccupy AA
20. Share information on a "need-to-know" basis

It may sound like a lot, but after reading this book and going through a few patrols, it will become second nature. I promise! Again, you've done this before. Often!

PASSAGE OF LINES

The patrol moves as one massed force. They periodically stop for many different reasons, and while stopped, patrols move forward of the massed force to conduct operations with the intention of shaping the battlefield for success.

This means patrols will depart through the forward line of troops (FLOT), and subsequently, they will be required to reenter the FLOT. This business of departing and reentering the FLOT is called the "passage of lines."

A passage of lines is a complex process at higher levels of command when the commander must move hundreds or even thousands of troops through the forward lines of another friendly unit. Obviously, when two friendly units converge upon the same space on a battlefield, there is always the potential to mistake each other for enemy. Fratricide is a very real danger in these cases, particularly at night!

For smaller tactical units, such as the fireteam, squad, and platoon, the process of departing and reentering the forward line is much simpler, though the danger of fratricide is the same. For this reason, coordinate carefully with the forward unit commander (FUC) and supporting unit commander (SUC). After all, the good guys shooting at each other is the last way to win.

Why Use This Tactic?

The process of a passage of lines serves as coordination between two units when one unit either moves forward or rearward through the defensive line of a stationary unit. More specifically, a unit may depart forward of the FLOT to maneuver against an enemy force. Conversely, a unit may reenter rearward of the FLOT to maneuver away from an enemy force.

Form the Team

The organization of the patrol depends more on the primary mission than on the passage of lines. The passage of lines is not a mission unto itself. It is merely a task to move toward or away from the enemy. Having said that, it is generally true that when conducting a passage of lines, the security team will move at the front of its formation to screen for enemy activity and protect the main patrol body.

Special Preparations

Passage of lines consists of essentially two tasks: (1) coordinating the time and place of *departure* and (2) coordinating the time, place, and signals of *reentry* through the FLOT. This means identifying a time and a passage point for both phases. The FUC identifies the passage lane, which is the precise route the patrol will take through his defensive position.

Use this flow chart for planning a passage of lines:
- Contact and coordinate with the FUC
- Move to an assembly area (AA) behind the passage point
- Link up with the guide to depart the FLOT
- Conduct a security halt past the forward edge of battle area (FEBA)
- Complete the mission
- Return to the passage point

The patrol forms into a tight 360-degree assembly area (AA) just behind the forward line of troops (FLOT). The patrol leader coordinates with the forward unit commander (FUC) for a guide through friendly forward obstacles, return routes, and times.

- Render the far and near recognition signal to the FUC
- Link up with the guide to reenter the FLOT
- Move into the AA to debrief the patrol

Copy this list onto a card (or carry this incredibly insightful book) and follow the list. It will soon become second nature.

By the Numbers!

Break it down into two parts: departing the FLOT and reentering the FLOT. The list will make sense once you begin to conceptualize the mission.

Departing the FLOT

1. Communicate and coordinate with the FUC. Coordinate the time and place of the patrol's departure and reentry. Choose an appropriate time. The FUC chooses the appropriate passage lane through his defenses. The FUC also assigns a guide to lead the patrol through the wire and mine obstacles of the FLOT.

2. Move to the AA behind the passage point. Here, the final planning, rehearsals, and coordination with the FUC takes place. For this coordination, the FUC supplies the following information:

   - An orientation on terrain
   - Known or suspected enemy positions
   - Recent enemy activity
   - The location of friendly OP/LP and obstacles—wire and minefields
   - Available combat support—guides, fire support, medevac, and reaction forces

   For coordination, the patrol supplies the following information to the FUC:

   - Unit designation
   - Patrol size
   - Departure and reentry times
   - All coordinating signals—near and far recognition

3. Link up with the guide to depart the FLOT through the passage lane. Once within the AA, the FUC links with the guide. Restate departure and reentry times and near and far recognition signals for the guide. Then introduce the guide to the patrol's point man and drag man. This allows the guide to recognize the patrol's beginning and end as he counts them through the passage lane.

The forward friendly unit (FFU) provides a guide through friendly obstacles—mines and wire. The guide waits at this position for a pre-determined length of time in case the patrol is engaged nearby and needs to fall back through the passage lane.

Also establish a time limit for which the guide will wait on the far side of the passage lane. This measure allows the guide to lead the patrol back through the passage lane if they are attacked in the FEBA and need to reenter the FLOT quickly!

4. Conduct a security halt past the FEBA. As soon as the patrol passes through the passage lane of the FLOT, they enter the FEBA. The patrol moves to the far side of the FEBA, seeks adequate concealment, and conducts a security halt. This first security halt is called the "listening halt." Every member of the patrol sits comfortably and then removes headgear. Making no noise, the patrol must listen to the sounds around them for about five minutes. This lets their eyes and ears adjust to the new environment.

5. Complete the mission. When the patrol is comfortable, feels safe, and has adjusted to the noises, sights, and smells around them, the patrol continues toward the objective. When the mission is complete, the patrol will return to the FLOT. Under normal circumstances, they return using a different route than they did on the advance. This reduces the opportunity for the enemy to ambush the patrol.

It might be worth mentioning here that, depending on the mission's nature, the patrol might not return to the FLOT, in which case, such coordination won't be necessary. Recognizing that exception, the norm is to always plan and coordinate for the return. Better safe than sorry, right?

Reentering the FLOT

1. Return to the passage point. The patrol returns to a secure position on the far side of the FEBA using a predetermined route. From this position, contact the FUC and coordinate to reenter the FLOT.

2. Render the far and near recognition signal to the FUC. Once in position, the patrol makes contact with the FUC/guide using the designated far recognition signal. The intention is to make contact with the far recognition signal first. Then, make contact using the near recognition signal. The far recognition signal uses distance signaling, such as a radio broadcast, smoke signal, or flare/light signal. The near recognition signal uses verbal contact, such as a password or visual recognition of each other.

   If, for any reason, the patrol cannot make contact with the far recognition signal, the patrol dispatches a small element forward to make contact with the FLOT using the near recognition signal to coordinate reentry. This is dangerous! This is not to be done during nighttime operations!

   During nighttime operations it is customary to wait in the security position until daylight, if the patrol cannot make contact with the FUC/guide using the far recognition signal. Only during daylight can the patrol render a near recognition signal without first making contact with the far recognition signal.

3. Link up with the guide to reenter the FLOT through the passage lane. After making contact with the FLOT, a security team crosses the FEBA to render the near recognition signal with the guide. A member of the security team then returns to the patrol and leads them across the FEBA to the guide waiting at the passage lane. The PL links up with the guide and counts the patrol members in *by name*. This lets the guide know that no enemy has slipped into the patrol and infiltrated their defensive line.

4. Move into the AA to debrief the patrol. The patrol moves back into the AA behind the FLOT. The PL and the FUC, or higher command, will debrief the patrol and discuss the nature and findings of the patrol on a "need–to–know basis."

Passage of lines is the coordination between two units when one unit must move forward or rearward through the defensive line of another unit. The patrol departs forward of the FLOT in order to maneuver against an enemy force and reenters rearward of the FLOT in order to maneuver away from an enemy force.

Essentially, departing and reentering the FLOT requires a coordination of (1) the time and place of departure and (2) the time, place, and signals of return. But, as you can see, these two seemingly simple requirements involve a complex understanding of the mission schedule. The patrol must be carefully planned, and the passage of lines must coordinate with the FUC.

Coordinating the departure and reentry of a patrol base follows an identical set of requirements. The only real difference is that the AA is really just the center of the patrol base, and the FUC is the commander. Otherwise, it all pretty much follows the same procedure.

CHAPTER 6
DEFENSIVE OPERATIONS

AREA DEFENSE

The area defense is the classic defensive line. It brings to mind images of the First World War, with a complex trench and bunker system, machine guns, artillery, and wire obstacles positioned well forward of the defensive line—in short, a static game of waiting.

In truth, a well-conducted area defense is anything but static. It's actually quite active and continues to advance its own fighting position while it patrols forward to gather intelligence on the enemy. The area defense has great depth and attempts to track and channel the enemy from considerable distances beyond the defense.

Why Use This Tactic?

Many tacticians insist that the area defense is only a temporary position. The intent of the area defense is to retain physical dominance over a given geographic location—however, *only to set the conditions favorable for attack.*

What does that mean? Defend so you can attack? Well, yes. If you are successful at repelling an enemy attack, the enemy has failed. Certainly, failure wasn't part of the enemy's plans, so it is safe to say the enemy is in some sort of disarray. Additionally, the enemy only quits the attack after they have spent significant resources. That means the enemy is in disarray *and* they are weak. Those are perfect conditions for counterattack.

Furthermore, even after the offensive maneuver has come to a halt, only assume a defensive posture *temporarily.* Once the patrol has massed its resources, rested, and re-supplied, it will again continue offensive operations.

So, the area defense is not a "decisive operation" because it does not thoroughly defeat the enemy. The area defense is a "shaping operation" that sets the conditions for success.

Form the Team

The area defense employs three teams and rotates those teams through the three tasked responsibilities—manning the line, manning the reserve, and patrolling forward. Remember, the area defense is rarely a short-term position, and troops must rest, be informed, and remain diligent. Necessarily, each team takes its turn conducting the three tasked responsibilities. For

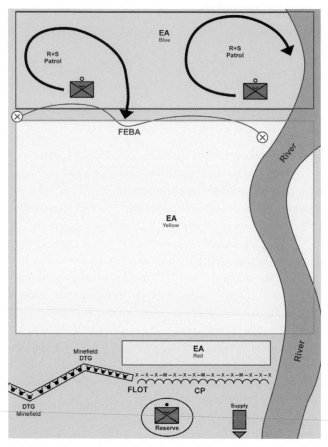

A defensive line secures its flanks by tying into another friendly unit, impassable terrain, or an obstacle, such as a minefield. R&S patrols screen in and forward of the FEBA to disrupt massing enemy. The reserve force can be deployed when necessary.

the sake of this chapter, let's call these teams "the reserve force," "the screening force," and "the line."

The line includes two-man fighting positions and crew-served weapon positions. It also includes the observation post/listening post (OP/LP) positioned just forward of the defensive line. Finally, while the command post (CP) is located behind the line near the reserve force, it is also part of the line force. The command team, however, does not rotate to the other assigned tasks, but a rest plan rotates among the command team members.

This organization permits the patrol to:

1. Maintain fifty percent of the force on the defensive line at all times
2. Maintain a reserve force of twenty-five percent to add depth to the position
3. Maintain a patrolling force of twenty-five percent forward to monitor enemy activity

The reserve and screening forces make up half of the total force for the area defense. The line force utilizes the other half of the troops. The troops are typically rotated in two-hour intervals—two hours on the line, two hours patrolling, two hours on the line again, and two hours in reserve where the troops can implement a sleep plan. In this manner, the patrol maintains defensive posture and still rests.

Special Preparations

Fire control measures are critical for the success of the area defense. These control measures help engage the attacking enemy at greater distances, synchronize the final defensive fire, and minimize the possibility of fratricide.

Place each fighting position so it has an interlocking **sector of fire** and every fighting position has supporting fire to its immediate front from the fighting positions to its left and right. This also ensures that no matter which section of the line the enemy attacks, three fighting positions will engage the enemy simultaneously!

Engagement areas indicate the location the commander intends to defeat the enemy and where the defensive line directs its fire. The goal is to employ weapons at the maximum range possible for the given terrain and diminish the enemy numbers

The defensive line is laid along a lazy "W"—not in a straight line. By staggering the line, depth is added to the defense, as well as flank protection because two or more positions may fire to the flanks at any given time.

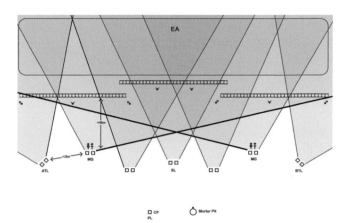

The engagement area (EA) is forward of the defensive obstacles. The effort here is to use the obstacles and/or terrain to slow or stop the enemy in the engagement area. Weapons interlock their fire to cover the obstacles and destroy the enemy.

before they are able to maneuver within hand-grenade range. For this reason, place wire obstacles and anti-personnel about fifty meters or more in front of the defensive line—just beyond hand-grenade range. This obstacle will slow the enemy in the last engagement area, allowing the patrol to execute its final protective fire and inflict massive casualties.

The **sector sketch** illustrates how each fighting position interlocks and how the left and right flanks of the defensive line are secured—by tying in with adjacent friendly units or using naturally occurring or man-made obstacles to stop the enemy approach. Additionally, the sector sketch identifies engagement areas, final protective fire, locations of wire and land-mine obstacles, the OP/LP, the CP, and assigned alternate fighting positions.

Finally, **engagement priorities** dictate which targets have the highest priority. These considerations may be assigned to individual weapon crews, such as assigning priority to armored vehicle targets for rocket crews, or commanders and radio operators to designated marksmen. Or, it may be assigned to everyone under general conditions, such as assigning priority to enemy combat engineers as they maneuver forward in an attempt to create gaps in wire obstacles.

By the Numbers!

The area defense forms the forward friendly line (FFL). Typically, the FFL defends against one direction in approximately a 120-degree frontal-fan that overlooks the designated engagement areas within the forward edge of battle area (FEBA).

Crew-served weapons, such as machine guns, rocket launchers, and mortars, serve as combat force multipliers. They add significant punch to fire within engagement areas (EA) and break up enemy attack formations. Their placement should be carefully considered.

1. Prior to moving up to the FEBA, the PL moves the patrol into a security halt at an appropriate distance. The PL will conduct a leader's recon of the FEBA and select the best location to establish a defensive line. The PL must issue a five-point contingency plan with the assistant patrol leader (APL) before leaving on the recon.

2. The PL moves up to the FEBA with at least a security team, which is placed in overwatch at the designated release point. This allows the PL to move more freely about the terrain and determine how best to place the defensive line. The leader's recon may require moving the entire recon team across the FEBA to consider possible avenues for an enemy attack.

3. Once the PL confirms or adjusts the plan, he gives the security team a five-point contingency plan and leaves them at the release point to monitor the FEBA. The PL returns to the patrol to disseminate any changes to the original plan.

4. Upon returning, the rest of the patrol forms into the line team, the reserve force, and the screening force. The order of march depends on the OPORD. The PL leads the patrol and links up with the security team at the release point.

5. After linking up with the security team, the PL designates the location of fighting positions for crew-served weapons and indicates their primary direction of fire. The PL then designates a CP at an appropriate distance behind the line, typically toward the center of the entire line. The PL designates an OP/LP location just forward of any wire obstacles and then designates a "fall back" position—an alternate position that can still cover the same engagement area within the FEBA.

6. The PL coordinates with units to his left and right to be certain he has adequately linked in with friendly defenses. Meanwhile, the team leaders disseminate to every member of the patrol the location of the CP, the OP/LP, and the alternate position.

7. At this point, the line team leader assigns each member a fighting position and a sector of fire to fill in the lazy "W." He ensures that all positions interlock with at least the position to their left and right. Fighting positions are two-man positions and are placed just close enough that they mutually support each other's immediate front. This distance varies according to different types of terrain. But, at a minimum, the positions must be able to cover forward obstacles with fire. Place land-mine and concertina-wire obstacles out of hand-grenade range (forty meters or more), within full view of friendly troops.

8. The reserve force locates behind the CP, out of sight from the line and out of the way of assigned indirect-fire crews. The reserve force familiarizes with the defensive line and the alternative position.

Once each position is set and assigned a sector of fire, communication devices are established at key locations—the command post (CP), flank positions, and observation post/listening post (OP/LP). Field telephones are more convenient than runners and more secure than radios.

9. Establish communication between key positions with field phones and landline wires. Field phones are more secure than radios and are not concerned with high traffic and frequency availability. Most field phones transmit a distance of several kilometers—ample distance for a defensive position.

10. At this point in the defense, the PL transitions to the forward unit commander (FUC). He collects the sector sketches from the team leaders to create his own master sketch and reports progress to higher command.

Priorities of Work

1. ***Security is always the first priority!*** The level of security varies significantly for the area defense but generally is no less than fifty percent—or as much as is required to man key positions, like crew-served weapons and the flanks.

2. An area defense continually develops its fighting positions. After all, positions are dug with adequate overhead cover, and communication trenches are dug from the CP to key positions. If the area defense remains for a long period of time, eventually all positions are connected by this trench system.

3. Equally as important to the defensive line is the continued screening of the FEBA that lies forward of the line. This is achieved to some degree within the defensive line and OP/LPs, but more likely, it will require the screening force to conduct recon and security (R&S) patrols forward into the FEBA and even beyond.

4. The reserve force leader implements a rest and maintenance plan to clean weapons, eat, and rest. This is critical because the reserve force is generally the only team allowed to sleep while serving on the defensive line.

The area defense retains dominance over a given geographical location, employing a fortified defensive line, a screening force, and a reserve force. Particular care is taken when coordinating and synchronizing fire control measures to repel any enemy attack.

While all three tasked responsibilities of the area defense are essential for success, the deployment of the reserve force—and therefore its very existence—is perhaps the single most critical factor for the area defense. The reserve force (1) reinforces the line when a breach is imminent or has already occurred, (2) adds depth by occupying alternate fighting positions to engage the enemy if line troops need to fall back, and (3) advances against a retreating enemy to fix the defeated enemy for counterattack.

As active as the area defense is, it is also sometimes tedious, even boring—more so in inclement weather. With rain or snow, the ground softens, and so does alertness of senses. Putting on heavier clothing further mutes the ability to see and hear an enemy force. It is an uncomfortable situation and perfect for enemy attack. Keeping troops vigilant and alert at these times is the challenge of excellent leadership.

Rotate the defensive line, the screening force, and the reserve force at least every two hours. No one can stay vigilant

Both natural and man-made obstacles are used to expose and/or slow the enemy advance in prepared engagement areas (EA). Troops use wire obstacles and place anti-personnel mines in defilades not covered by fire.

The reserve force is perhaps the single most decisive element of the defense. The reserve may counterattack, reinforce a failing line, or occupy a secondary defensive position. It is typically placed near the command post (CP) out of the enemy's line of sight so the enemy will not know when the reserve force commits to battle.

much longer than that. Rotation allows all troops to get periodic rest. Furthermore, taking part in the R&S patrols forward of the defensive line gives the troops an excellent idea of where the threat will approach and how best to continue developing their defenses.

MOBILE DEFENSE

The mobile defense takes its roots from guerilla warfare tactics and has significant application in counterinsurgency (COIN) operations. Rather than face a formidable enemy head-on, its intention is to deny enemy access to a given territory by means of an active, dynamic defense. The mobile defense will attack the enemy force through asymmetrical battle. Supply routes and rear-echelon troops of the offense are the primary targets for the mobile defense. However—make no mistake—the defeat of the enemy's combat force is the ultimate goal. When relatively certain of victory, the mobile defense will stand and fight toe-to-toe with the combat troops of any offensive force!

Mobile defenses place a great deal of emphasis on *mobility*, *flexibility*, and *communication*. In this manner, a relatively small force can defend a sizable amount of terrain that would otherwise be impossible to achieve with an area defense.

Why Use This Tactic?

The mobile defense realizes *they* are the enemy's ultimate objective. In this case, the enemy does not seek to gain terrain or facilities or even population centers, per se. The enemy seeks the destruction and elimination of the guerilla force. Oddly, this realization can be very liberating.

The mobile defense is "liberated" from defending terrain. Within the paradigm of guerilla warfare, terrain has very little, fleeting value. Since it holds such little value, troops should not be unnecessarily "spent" for terrain.

Form the Team

You're not likely to see long, elaborate defensive lines in a mobile defense. It's not that the mobile defense is exclusive of the area defense. Far from it! The mobile defense utilizes *all* of the principal elements of the area defense—concealed fighting positions, coordinated sectors of fire, obstacles to slow or stop the enemy within sectors of fire, established lines of communication, secondary lines of defense, and a reserve force. Everything.

However, instead of being a long-running defensive line, the mobile defense makes use of multiple *defensive perimeters*. The mobile defensive perimeters are carefully networked together for communication purposes and assigned priority

The mobile defense does not seek to hold key terrain unless such terrain offers a decisive defeat against an enemy attack. Even then, key terrain is held only temporarily. Mobile defenses protect resources, such as communication nodes, using forward operating bases (FOB).

status, with each perimeter possessing a reserve force to act as a quick reaction force (QRF). The QRF from each mobile defensive perimeter can be called into action for the defense of other local defensive perimeters.

Priority Status

Each defensive perimeter gets a priority status. Reserve "top priority" for those positions that *must be held*—such as a major command HQ, communication site, or supply cache. Since all other defensive perimeters with a lower priority status must come to the aid of this type of perimeter, be careful not to issue this status to any defensive perimeter that is not absolutely necessary! Otherwise, valuable troops are lost for insignificant terrain.

A "mid-priority" status defensive perimeter is reserved for those positions that, while offering nothing of strategic value, offer the greatest opportunity for victory. If the defeat of an enemy offensive is highly likely, assign this perimeter mid-level priority status. Any defensive perimeter with an equal or lesser priority status can help defend this perimeter.

A "low-priority" status defensive perimeter is assigned to positions serving merely as troop stations. These defensive perimeters serve only to advance the network of defense by pressing out combat operations into further territory. Accordingly, these perimeters receive a low priority, since they will simply be abandoned upon an enemy attack. Only defend the defensive perimeters if enemy defeat is certain. In such a case, its priority status may be elevated accordingly.

Intervals

Frankly, there is no hard and fast rule on how far apart defensive perimeters are from one another. Such considerations are completely situational and depend on considerations of *M*ission, *E*nemy, *T*errain and weather, *T*ime available, *T*roops available, and *C*ivilians on the battlefield (METT-TC). Still, the goal is that each defensive perimeter have the ability to dispatch the reserve force to come to the immediate aid of another defensive perimeter in their area. This is particularly true if that other is of equal or higher priority.

Special Preparations

The mobile defense defeats the enemy offensive through the expert use of local terrain and the deployment of a highly mobile reserve force.

Now, a prevailing opinion remains in military circles that "the defense is not decisive because it does not exert its will over its enemy." Yes, yes . . . and a counterattack is not truly a defensive posture, but an offensive one instead. Those are academic arguments best left to the heated discussions of general officers over coffee and cheesecake.

The fact is that the mobile defense organizes and deploys with the intent of defeating its enemy in decisive battle. As such, it makes use of the local terrain and a mobile reserve.

Local Terrain

Genghis Kahn was able to lure defenders out of their positions to "finish off" his so-called wounded enemy force—only to find themselves trapped in the kill zone of Kahn's larger enemy force. In much the same way, lure an offensive force into your kill zones. And it should be easy, since the offensive force is looking for something to attack.

Look for terrain that channels the attacking force, permits an advantageous placement of fighting positions to attack by fire, and allows the patrol to behave as an effective screening force. Most people will think of ravines, and that's good, but what if your terrain doesn't have ravines? What if your terrain is predominately flat?

In those cases, pay close attention to tree lines. The advancing enemy will likely skirt around tree lines because trees offer some semblance of cover and concealment. Also, look at creeks and washes where there is plenty of erosion. This will create natural low points the enemy may advance through. Finally, look at high-speed avenues of approach. Even in an open field, the enemy will want to advance along the most certain path. Roads and paths offer harder surfaces. Remember, the enemy often acts like water. They seek the path of least resistance. This is true even for thorn thickets and swamps. Use the edges of these natural obstacles because the enemy will want to skirt around them to avoid walking *through* them!

Once you have determined the most likely enemy approach, you must establish your fighting positions so that your defense can take the greatest advantage of its vantage point. You will want to create the best sectors of fire into the enemy approach.

Establish OP/LP along this avenue of approach. Be sure that your R&S teams monitor these possible approaches. If they detect enemy reconnaissance teams moving along these paths, the R&S teams should be prepared to ambush them to prevent the enemy from obtaining information regarding the defensive perimeter.

In this manner, use the terrain to (1) establish defensive perimeters, (2) channel the enemy into the patrol's sectors of fire, (3) gather intelligence on the enemy disposition, and (4) deny the enemy any information on the patrol's defenses. Finally, use the terrain to counterattack a retreating enemy in the terrain chokepoints.

Each position in a mobile defense is assigned a priority. Those with the higher priority are aided when under enemy attack by counterattacks from lower-priority positions' reserve forces. When low-priority positions are attacked, troops should covertly withdraw.

Mobile Reserve

The reserve force is the hammer of the mobile defense's "hammer and anvil" tactic. It must be incredibly mobile, which means that it will often include smaller teams—perhaps a fireteam or squad. This reserve force must be ready to move on a moment's notice, communicate while crossing challenging terrain, and jump right into the fight!

The defensive perimeter under attack serves as the anvil. This defense has already found the enemy and fixed them to a fight. We can anticipate the enemy attacking force will significantly outnumber the troops in the defensive perimeter. They would be foolish to attack with less than 3:1 odds.

This means the defensive perimeter's own reserve force is most likely still operating *inside* the perimeter attempting to hold back the attacking force. However, if the defensive perimeter has been breached, their reserve force is most likely operating *outside* of the perimeter. Now, the mobile reserve force must coordinate with the reserve force of the defensive perimeter to avoid "friendly fire." Additionally, if more than one mobile reserve force is called up from adjacent local defensive perimeters, these forces must also be coordinated.

The main effort of the mobile reserve force is to catch the enemy from the rear or flanks, still trapped inside those channeled avenues of approach. This is where the enemy attack is most vulnerable. The enemy will not be prepared to conduct an offensive operation to their front, rear, and flanks. This is virtually impossible. So, the mobile reserve force must conduct counterattacks almost immediately to force the enemy to disengage from their assault.

Think of this like walking into a spider web. What happens when you walk between two trees and get a face full of spider web? It wraps around your head, falls onto your shoulders, and before you know it, you have spider web all over you. *That* is what the mobile reserve force should feel like to the enemy attack force.

As the enemy withdraws along its avenue of attack, the mobile reserve will continue to attack them. With the offense retreating, the enemy is not in a strong position to defend. With multiple and well-coordinated reserve forces, the enemy may be defeated along their avenues of approach/retreat.

By the Numbers!

The mobile defensive perimeter is established much in the same way as a patrol base—using the triangle method. The difference between a mobile defense and a patrol base is that the mobile defensive perimeter will be used for a lengthy time. While intentionally hidden from enemy detection, the development of advanced fighting positions and obstacles more closely resembles a defensive line than the temporary defenses of the patrol base.

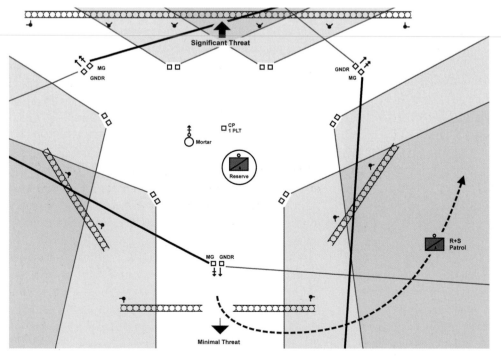

The mobile defense uses multiple defensive perimeters, or forward operating bases (FOB), networked together for mutual support. Otherwise, all the principles of the area defense are employed—obstacles, coordinated fire, R&S patrols, and a reserve force.

1. Obstacles—preferably wire obstacles—are placed completely around the perimeter, in front of all three of the triangle's sides. Anti-personnel mines are carefully placed and marked on each squad's sector sketch.

2. Communication—preferably a field phone—is established at each of the apexes and back to the CP in the center. The wire is hung and camouflaged in the trees or buried underground. Additionally, communication is established with adjacent defensive perimeters.

3. Crew-served weapons, such as mortars or recoilless rifles, are located near the CP, while machine-gun crews are located at each of the three apexes. Here the reserve force rests, eats, and carries out other duties.

4. OP/LP or R&S patrols are sent out in irregular patterns to obtain intelligence on enemy movement in the immediate area. Additionally, these patrols are intended to thwart the enemy's effort to gain information regarding the size, activity, and location of the defensive perimeter.

5. Coordinated secondary sectors of fire are designated so each of the fighting positions can *fire in toward the center* of the defensive perimeter. Only perform this drastic measure if one of the defensive lines of the triangle is breached and the CP abandoned. A designated signal indicates that the CP has withdrawn, issuing the "commence fire" order to the other two lengths of the defensive perimeter. The advantage of such a drastic measure is that it adds depth to the defense because the remaining two lines can fire upon the enemy attack force as they attempt to clear and reorganize on their objective—the now-abandoned line of one side of the defensive triangle. This measure allows the other two lines of the defensive triangle to take the enemy under fire from two directions!

6. In the event one line of the triangle is overrun, the reserve force also withdraws with the command team. This frees the reserve force to conduct counterattacks against the enemy's flank or rear—from directions the enemy is ill-prepared to fight.

The mobile defense *can* deliver a decisive victory! It takes a *flexible* defense network, a *mobile* reserve force, and excellent *communication* (C4ISR). The greatest emphasis must be placed on coordinating and mobilizing those reserve forces. Active patrolling will be the only means for determining when and where the enemy will attack.

The mobile defense *does not* abandon the lessons and principles of the area defense. These elements are applied to the mobile defense as well—though in a very different manner and to a different effect. When used in conjunction with the swarming attack, the mobile defense is a significant tactic within COIN operations.

The mobile defense is dynamic and often unorthodox. Standoff elements—such as mines, IED, mortars, and rockets—are used to threaten enemy activity. Anti-personnel and vehicle mines are used to deter enemy patrols.

CHAPTER 7
OFFENSIVE OPERATIONS

MOVEMENT TO CONTACT

The Movement to Contact (MTC) is a primary form of offensive operation. It offers the commander an alternative to the attack. It is used when *little is known* about the enemy disposition.

Because little is known about the enemy's location, defenses, size, or activity, the MTC is controlled in one of two ways—dedicated to either an axis of advance (as marked on a map) or to the destruction of an identified enemy force. The commander receives greater leeway in movement when the MTC is dedicated to the destruction of an enemy force. However, regardless of whether the MTC seeks an identified enemy or is ordered to clear an axis of advance, the MTC includes established boundaries to prevent fratricide or overextending the patrol.

Why Use This Tactic?

The MTC seeks to engage and destroy the enemy and/or clear areas of enemy presence. This is much more challenging than it sounds, given that your force does not really have much information on the enemy's whereabouts. MTC is often performed like a game of tag in the dark. The goal is to locate the enemy, decide whether to deploy the reserve, engage the enemy, destroy, or route the enemy force. Intelligence develops continually and "on the fly."

"*See First. Understand First. Act First. Finish Decisively.*" That is the mantra of the U.S. Army's Future Force. This is also an excellent list of requirements for the commander of an MTC.

See First

The trick is to locate the enemy. This does not have to be done quickly, but your forces must locate the enemy before they locate you! You will not have a great deal of intelligence regarding the enemy disposition. If you *did* have this information, you wouldn't be conducting a MTC but, rather, conducting an attack. However, the enemy probably has *even less* information regarding your force. Even when they finally detect your force, it is unlikely they will immediately understand your intentions. Make this work to your advantage. Find the enemy *first*.

Finding the enemy is the job of the vanguard. The vanguard is deployed in multiple teams, forward of the main body/reserve force. In this way, the vanguard behaves as a force reconnaissance team, pulling the main body/reserve toward the essential enemy objectives while simply bypassing and isolating smaller, insignificant enemy positions.

Understand First

Just because one of your vanguard units bumps into an enemy OP/LP doesn't mean all is lost. Remember, the enemy has little intelligence about your mission. They probably don't even know *why* you are in their area . . . yet. So, it is very important that your vanguards continue to act as "force recon," frequently giving the commander information regarding enemy activity in their sectors.

With this information, you must decide if it is necessary to engage the enemy or bypass the enemy. If you will engage, can the enemy be defeated with just the vanguard, or will the reserve force need to be dedicated to the fight?

Because movement to contact (MTC) is used when the patrol has little information on the enemy situation, multiple vanguard teams are dispatched forward of the main body. The information passed back from the vanguards helps the commander decide where to focus the main attack force.

Obviously, it is critical that the commander of the MTC understand:
1. What his vanguard force is fighting
2. Whether to commit the reserve or simply bypass the enemy

Act First

Seek the initiative. Keep the enemy off balance and continue to press until they have fled, or the MTC has destroyed them. Work with the smallest force possible. If the vanguard can destroy the enemy alone, let them do so. If not, either deploy the reserve force or bypass the enemy if they are not the decisive objective.

Dedicating the reserve force is critical. The MTC relies greatly on your momentum forward to clear the territory or pursue the enemy. Your momentum depends greatly on your ability to keep the enemy off balance, which means the enemy is unable to coordinate a defense or counterattack. So, if you dedicate the reserve force to a fight that is unnecessary, you're allowing the enemy time to coordinate and react.

If one of your vanguard teams can engage and destroy a small enemy unit, then do so promptly. Otherwise, bypass this small force and isolate them. But be warned, if your vanguard forces become tied down to independent engagements, then they can no longer push information back to the main body/reserve force of the MTC. That would stall your momentum and leave the reserve blind—not good.

Finish Decisively

The MTC is a primary offensive operation. If all goes well, the MTC will either clear the assigned axis of advance, destroy the enemy, or both. And, with the vanguard acting in the role of force reconnaissance, often you will have a better grasp of the enemy disposition at the end of the mission. With this information, you may wish to transition into a follow-up offensive operation, such as the exploitation or pursuit for further tactical and operational gain.

That is what "finish decisively" means. The MTC must defeat the enemy so they are unprepared to conduct coordinated combat operations against your force. Furthermore, your force should be in a position to regroup and quickly transition into another combat operation. If the enemy is unable to keep up with your force's tempo, they will soon lose their will to fight.

Form the Team

The commander will remain with the main body of the MTC. Other than the command team, the reserve force makes up the main body. The reserve force typically consists of approximately fifty percent of the force. This is because the MTC is conducted when little is known about the enemy disposition. Having a large reserve force gives the commander considerable power when committing the reserve force to a battle.

The MTC also makes use of multiple vanguard teams. Typically, at least two forward vanguards are used, and three vanguards are preferred. Whether you form into two or three vanguard teams, the total vanguard force equals approximately half of the total number of troops for the MTC. So, if there are two vanguards, each team equals approximately twenty-five percent of the total force. If there are three vanguards, each team equals about fifteen percent of the total force.

The vanguard teams should be light and mobile but still carry enough armament to engage and destroy an enemy force of equal size. The primary mission of the vanguard is to conduct reconnaissance. The team leader must continually transmit information on enemy activity in the area of the vanguard team. If the vanguard team becomes decisively engaged, then it is unable to continue reconnaissance.

Therefore, while a vanguard team must be *able* to engage and defeat the enemy, it is desirable that the vanguard team simply report the enemy's disposition. Ideally, the vanguard should wait for reinforcements from the reserve force or wait until the MTC commander orders their assault of the enemy. However, once under fire, the vanguard team must conduct itself in a manner to preserve the team.

Special Preparations

It will be difficult to plan for every contingency that might occur during an MTC, since so little is known about the enemy disposition. Still, there are some battlefield preparations that will aid the MTC in its success.

First and foremost, study the **terrain map** of the territory in which the MTC will be conducted. Having a solid idea of the terrain not only allows the patrol to maneuver more effectively, it also helps to identify **named areas of interest** (NAI) where the enemy is likely to mass, defend, or escape through. These NAI can be numbered on the map in the order of their priority.

Identify the **left and right boundaries**, as well as the **start point** (SP) and forward-most **limit of advance** (LOA). This will keep the MTC patrol focused, even if an enemy force is identified as the objective rather than an axis of advance. It will also keep the patrol from entering the axis of an adjacent unit, limiting the risk of friendly fire incidents.

With the vanguard force patrolling forward, communication is key to relaying information back to the commander with the main body of the MTC. The vanguard teams continue to develop the situation and send timely reports. The main body follows behind as the commander dictates.

Multiple **phase lines** will establish the progress of the MTC patrol as it continues to press the enemy. This also makes for ease of reference for the commander and vanguard team leaders when discussing enemy positions or movements.

Last, identify anticipated **en-route rally points** (ERP) after the SP and each phase line. These should be approximated at points on the map that appear to be easily defended terrain.

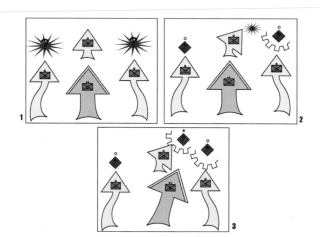

The movement to contact (MTC) uses multiple vanguard teams to find the enemy. When a vanguard makes contact, they report the information. Often, more than one vanguard is in contact with the enemy. The commander must choose the enemy force against which to commit his main force.

By the Numbers!

1. The commander conducts a final communication check with the vanguard teams and dispatches them forward of the main body. The commander starts movement of the main body, keeping a distance great enough to avoid becoming absorbed when a vanguard team engages the enemy and yet close enough to respond quickly with the reserve force.

2. Each vanguard team seeks visual contact with the enemy, being careful not to engage in a firefight. If the vanguard team enters a firefight with the enemy, the PL loses the mobility necessary to develop the situation and collect intelligence for the commander. If the vanguard becomes decisively engaged, the PL reports information back to the commander with the main body.

3. The commander assesses the information coming from the vanguard force in contact with the enemy to determine if the main body should commit to attacking the enemy body, if the vanguard team can effectively attack the enemy force, or if the enemy body should simply be bypassed.

4. The vanguard team in contact with the enemy acts as a **shaping operation**, meaning the vanguard team doesn't conduct the main attack. Instead, the vanguard fixes the enemy using an attack by fire to suppress and isolate the enemy force until the reserve force can maneuver to destroy them. Alternatively, the vanguard team can be instructed to attack and destroy any smaller enemy force that presents a threat to the main body's flank or rear. Even in this case, the vanguard functions as a shaping operation within the force-protection framework.

5. If the commander determines the main body needs to eliminate the detected enemy, he directs or leads the reserve force to crush the fixed enemy. This becomes the **decisive operation**, meaning it becomes the main attack. It consumes the attention and resources of the MTC until the engagement is concluded. If necessary, the commander pulls the other vanguard teams into the attack, attempting to isolate each subsequent enemy force so the enemy cannot coordinate their actions.

6. Once the engagement concludes, the commander again dispatches his vanguard teams forward and continues the movement—either to clear an axis of movement or to defeat an identified enemy force. In any case, it is critical that the vanguard seek and maintain visual contact with the enemy force and continue to develop the situation for the MTC commander.

Once the commander has determined one of the vanguard forces is in contact with a key enemy element or terrain, the main body of the MTC is committed to the battle. The vanguard force fixes the enemy position while the main body attacks aggressively.

ATTACK

How do you break an egg? Just hit the shell at one point, and the entire shell cracks open. Simple enough, but why not just squeeze the egg in your hands? Would it break? Honestly, no.

An eggshell is very strong. Its shell is arched and can withstand pressure hundreds and even thousands of times its own weight! The only reason the eggshell *appears* to be fragile is because you use a small amount of mass—like the edge of the skillet—to penetrate a very small portion of the entire eggshell.

In the human endeavor of warfare, defenses are very similar to the eggshell. The defense's fighting positions mutually support each other. Attacking along the full surface of the defense, the total attacking force will have to outnumber the enemy's defense *3 to 1, minimum.* Even then, the advantages of modern weapon systems can negate superior numbers. In short, victory is not guaranteed.

So, when conducting an attack, the commander must know the best location to hit the enemy's defense. Then, mass the attack forces, assault the enemy line at their most vulnerable point, and exploit the gap, sending in more troops to continue the attack. In this way, the enemy's defensive line will soon fall to pieces like the eggshell. However, to achieve this requires significant information from reconnaissance assets.

Reconnaissance is important because, without adequate information, the force should never conduct an attack. Instead, knowing very little about the enemy, the force should use another form of offensive tactic to engage, such as MTC.

Why Use This Tactic?

The attack is a primary form of offensive operation seeking to impose will through either decisive defeat or seizure of essential terrain or facilities. This requires mass, mobility, and the element of surprise.

Massing combat power—troops, weapons, and fire—is a luxury the defense does not have. The defense must distribute combat power over the larger area it intends to defend. True, these resources are coordinated to support one another, but there isn't a great deal of flexibility in the defense's use of combat power unless the defense is willing to surrender valuable territory or facilities.

The attack masses and focuses combat power against the enemy's spread-out resources. This is why an attack *doesn't need* to outnumber the defending force. The patrol only needs to outnumber the defending enemy *at the point of local contact.*

The armies of the First World War learned at a very costly price that it is best for a small attack force to create the initial gap in the enemy line and then to exploit that gap by filling in larger numbers of troops. Such a tactic requires the attack to use mobility and surprise to hide the exact location of the planned assault.

Form the Team

The attack force breaks into two teams—the support team and the assault team. If the enemy is specifically known to have prior warning of attack *and* is known to have the available resources to conduct spoiling attacks, the force's attack may also form a security team for protecting its flanks. Otherwise, the attack uses just the support and assault teams.

The support team masses together combat power in weaponry. The support team employs machine guns, grenade launchers, and rockets to suppress enemy defenses while the assault team moves forward to destroy key positions.

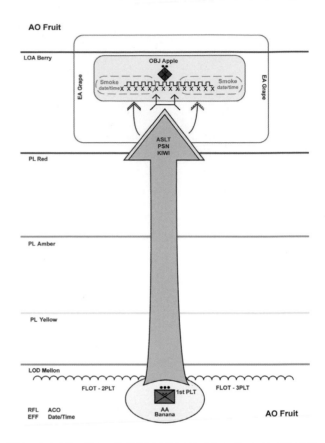

The progression of an attack takes the patrol from the assembly area through an attack lane up to the assault position. The support team deploys first. Note the feign attack to the right and actual attack to the left are masked by smoke.

The assault team includes an internal breach team tasked with the responsibility of cutting a path through the enemy's forward obstacles. This team typically consists of a two-man security team and a two-man engineer team. The breach team carries specialized equipment for cutting through wire, neutralizing land mines, and marking the path they have created through breach in the enemy's obstacles. In most cases, the breach team will require an ample number of smoke canisters to mask their activity.

The support team employs mass-casualty-producing weapons and may also have an internal sub-team to conduct a feign attack. The feign attack is coordinated to advance at the same time as the breach team advances. The feign attack pulls attention away from the breach team to confuse the enemy about the true location of the main assault force.

Like the breach team, the feign attack team employs smoke canisters and high rates of fire to make their attack look convincing, though the feign attack team would rarely attempt to pass through the enemy obstacles. Instead, the feign attack team remains just outside the wire obstacle and conducts an attack by fire to augment the main support team's base of fire.

Special Preparations

The patrol leader uses the commander's intent to develop the attack plan. The principles of *M*ission, *E*nemy, *T*errain and weather, *T*ime available, *T*roops available, and *C*ivilians on the battlefield (METT-TC) are considered and influence the attack plan's scheme of maneuver and fire support. Control measures are implemented to ensure that friendly fire incidents do not occur.

Using a map overlay, the patrol leader identifies the ***movement control measures***, such as the assembly area (AA), the line of departure (LD), the axis of advance, the phase lines, the assault position, the objective (OBJ), and the limit of advance (LOA). Furthermore, the larger area of operations (AO) is indicated, giving special attention to any friendly unit's location and activity.

Using a map overlay, the patrol leader identifies the ***fire control measures***, such as the engagement area (EA), the target reference points (TRP), the direction of fire, and the restrictive fire line (RFL). In addition to those terrain-based fire control measures, the PL delineates the threat-based fire control measures. At a minimum, these include the engagement priorities, rules of engagement (ROE), and weapon safety postures.

By the Numbers!

In the event your patrol is tasked to conduct an attack, you will go through a nine-step process for the planning and execution of actions on the objective. It's unlikely that your patrol will avoid any step of this procedure. Familiarize yourself with it and bookmark this page.

1. **Move to the assault position**. An assault position is the last covered and concealed position before the OBJ. It differs from an ORP in that the patrol will *not* return to the assault position. The patrol is not required to stop in the assault position, but it is common to wait there so friendly units and supporting fire can synchronize against the enemy target. A leader's recon of the objective is optional, but with good intelligence, this is not required.

2. **Form the attack**. At the designated time, the PL forms the patrol into its attack formation and order of march. This is the start of the attack. The patrol bypasses all obstacles not assigned specifically to it unless they present a threat. Pass through danger areas keeping in the attack formation. Expose only as large a force as necessary to achieve each task. This conceals the size and intent of the patrol's attack.

3. **Identify the OBJ**. The point man determines the direction and distance of the OPFOR position (the OBJ) and leads the support team to its assigned position. This position allows the support team to observe the OPFOR defensive line and employ suppressive fire if the enemy detects the attack.

4. **Engage the OBJ**. The support team *does not* indiscriminately fire upon the OPFOR position if it still has the element of surprise! The assault's breach team moves up to the objective to neutralize the enemy's obstacles. If the attack is detected, the support team employs suppressive fire against the OPFOR fighting positions.

5. **Breach obstacles**. Using the lowest available terrain for cover, the assault's breach team moves forward. If the support team is not firing, the breach team uses stealth in approaching its objective. If suppressive fire is already underway, the breach team employs smoke to mask their movement. Simultaneously, the support team's feign attack employs a smoke screen at another point along the enemy's defensive line and attacks by fire. This will confuse the OPFOR as to the location of the breach team. The breach team uses visual tape during the day, or lights at night, to mark the breach of the enemy's obstacles.

6. **Exploit the breach**. The breach team signals the assault leader once they have opened a path through the obstacles. Using the breach team as near-side security and moving under the cover fire of the support team, the entire assault team moves quickly through the breach.

7. **Clear the objective**. The assault team uses high-volume fire and a small maneuver force to clear the first couple of fighting positions. Fireteams are assigned specific tasks, such as taking out bunkers or providing for left and right security. The support team continues to shift fire as the

The assault team further breaks down into a breach team and a support team. As its name implies, the breach team has the un-enviable job of moving forward to neutralize enemy obstacles. They intentionally look for defilades and use smoke to obscure their exact location.

Once the breach team opens a path through enemy obstacles, the rest of the assault team moves forward aggressively to destroy key enemy positions. The support team continues to suppress the enemy with high-volume fire during this period.

assault team clears more enemy fighting positions. The support team must keep the OPFOR suppressed and unable to form a counterattack. When the assault team clears enough of the OPFOR positions, the assault leader signals for the support team to move through the breach and join the assault team. Now the patrol attacks assigned targets—such as the OPFOR, CP, and communications nodes—or it may continue to attack the enemy's exposed flanks.

8. **Reconsolidate and reorganize**. To regain the patrol's mass and strength, the PL forms the patrol into a 180-degree security position on the far side of the OBJ and prepares for a counterattack. Element leaders use liquid, ammo, casualties, equipment (LACE) considerations to account for personnel, ensure key weapon systems are manned, and redistribute ammo and water. The PL reports to higher command the progress of the attack and coordinates for supporting resources. Friendly casualties are evacuated, as are POWs, according to the OPORD. In truth, reconsolidation and reorganization may occur even before all the objectives have been accomplished. It is an ongoing task.

9. **Continue the mission**. After seizing the OBJ, the patrol prepares to transform into a new mission and might defend, withdraw, or begin an exploitation or pursuit.

The following considerations will help avoid common mistakes made during an attack.

- **Use stealth until contact has been made**. Do not run when a slow, steady pace will do. A slow pace is unnerving, particularly for the PL. However, the lead fireteam must be allowed to look carefully for the OPFOR, OP/LP, land mines, and other obstacles. It is to the patrol's advantage to see the OPFOR first!

- **Do not break your attack formation for danger areas**. The attack formation provides the patrol with enough security to move through most danger areas.

- **Bypass all unassigned obstacles**. However, *mark* all obstacles clearly. Visible markings allow follow-on friendly units to neutralize these obstacles later.

- **Use only the force necessary to complete a task**. Do not deploy the entire patrol against an OPFOR position if only one or two fireteams are needed.

- **React with violence once contact has been made**. The patrol grabs the OPFOR by their belts and hangs on! You may feel momentary relief when the enemy runs away, but the OPFOR is only repositioning to get a better shot at your patrol. Do not allow the OPFOR to fall back and coordinate their efforts. Gain contact with the enemy, attack violently until the enemy flees, and regain contact.

There are numerous actions to conduct on the objective —breaching obstacles, destroying key positions, and reconsolidating for enemy counterattack. Seizing enemy prisoners, weapons, and intelligence are also essential tasks.

Keep up the momentum of forward movement.

The attack is potentially the most lethal of all combat missions. The weapons of the modern battlefield are devastating. Coordination of fire and maneuver is a daunting task.

The U.S. Army's top field archivist, General S. L. A. Marshall, described the modern battlefield as "organized chaos." Though Marshall coined that phrase half a century ago, it is no less true today. Organized chaos describes the dynamic characteristics of the battlefield. This chaos cannot be controlled but can be directed toward a common goal. The problem is that no two people will have the same perspective of the raging battle, and yet somehow, they must communicate over the chaos and work toward that common goal.

The battle will task the commander on the ground with more responsibilities than he will ever be able to meet. The only hope for success is to prioritize the tasks as they become pertinent—a triage of responsibilities. On the battlefield this is an art form.

Exploitation operations seek to gain enemy terrain, facilities, and resources. The seizure of weapon and ammunition caches is a legitimate exploitation goal because it denies the enemy valuable resources.

There is no "silver bullet"—no single factor for success. Battle is chaotic. Soldiers *need* to know what is expected of them. The worst thing a leader could do is send a troop marching and not tell him how far he is going. Everyone fears the unknown. Confidence is hammered out in the OPORD and effective rehearsals. *Be certain your troops are informed!*

EXPLOITATION

The exploitation is a follow-up form of attack that seeks to gain territory, key facilities, or enemy resources like supply caches. However, exploitation is not a primary form of attack. That means the exploitation will follow a successful attack, MTC, or defense. It may be planned as a branch or sequel to any of these missions.

The exploitation will require a defined objective, which means terrain or facility. Additionally, like the MTC, exploitation relies on the experience of the leadership to know when to bypass the enemy, when to engage the enemy, and how to recognize signs of culmination—a point when the mission will bear no more success.

Why Use This Tactic?

The expressed intention of the exploitation is to seize land or structures by capitalizing on the success of the prior mission—thereby making the exploitation mission an opportunistic venture. By following up tactical success with further tactical success, operational gains may be achieved.

Form the Team

Exploitation is rarely planned into the initial phases of a mission, though it should be considered a branch or a sequel of the larger operation. As such, it would be rare indeed to have so many troops that commanders could organize an entire reserve force into an exploitation mission. Far more likely, they will have to transition the force from the preceding mission into exploitation.

Transitioning to exploitation from an MTC mission would be the easiest of all, since the exploitation looks and acts very much the same way. The only difference is that, while an MTC may be committed to an objective within a given zone, enemy population, or condition, the exploitation seeks an objective with a more precise geographical location. This gives the commander greater leeway in deciding to bypass or engage enemy pockets of resistance.

Transitioning to exploitation from an attack takes a little more effort. Again, the exploitation forms up very much like an MTC where the main body/reserve force is likely to include fifty percent or more of the force, with multiple vanguards to act as a screening force. The attack, by contrast, has a very small reserve and vanguard. However, the attack also maintains a large main body.

Once an attack has successfully breached a defensive line, reorganized on the objective, and determined the enemy is falling back, it will have to transition quickly to take advantage of the enemy's present state of disarray. In that time, the enemy is most vulnerable, making the objective of the exploitation ripe for the picking!

Whatever the transition method, the commander will have discussed this possibility with his subordinate leaders as part of the previous mission plan. Whether the assault force assumes the role of vanguard while the security and support teams form into the main body, or vice-versa, the commander will communicate the *planned method* and the *new objective* quickly.

Finally, transitioning to exploitation from defense may also present a dilemma. The rule of thumb says never, never, never abandon the defensive line to charge forward. If you adhere to that doctrine in the strictest sense, the best you could do would be to dispatch your reserve force to conduct the exploitation in hopes of seizing the objective.

However, there is another tactical opinion that says something to the effect of "don't defend when it is unnecessary," meaning that if, after repelling the enemy, it is in your best interest to move your force forward to seize additional land or structures, then do it! Move your reserve force forward into a vanguard force and form your defensive line into a large main body/reserve force. Then press forward in exploitation of previous success.

Special Preparations

Since the exploitation is, as previously stated, a follow-up attack and not a primary offensive operation, it is difficult to prepare specifically for the possibility of exploitation. However, at the very root of the exploitation mission is knowing exactly *what* will be seized.

A commander must describe for subordinate leaders:

- Their assigned role if the current mission presents an opportunity for exploitation
- The conditions in which exploitation would be favorable
- The assigned objective(s)

To designate an objective requires some type of forward reconnaissance to determine the location of the objective, routes to the objective, and the lay of the land at the objective. Know the immediate enemy threat after seizing the objective and be certain the force is capable of repelling any enemy attempt to regain terrain or facilities.

By the Numbers!

Plan exploitation as a branch or sequel to another combat operation. It is difficult to detail the exact execution because much depends on the primary operation. However, exploitation's goal is to seize enemy terrain, facilities, or resources. The exact target of the exploitation may not become clear until the first operation has achieved its objectives.

1. The commander and subordinate leaders must know what lies ahead. As the force conducts exploitation, it commonly bypasses small pockets of enemy resistance because the destruction of the enemy force is *not* the objective. Instead, focus on property seizure. Bypass anything that does not present a threat to rear or flanks.

2. If not possible to bypass, the commander may chose to isolate the enemy and continue to press the exploitation. The commander may also choose to destroy the enemy precisely, as done in an MTC. In any case, do not leave an enemy force behind capable of striking either the exploitation force or sustainment force.

3. Last, the commander must be aware of culmination signs. Those signs include the seizure of all objectives, troop exhaustion, ammunition or water shortages, or losing more engagements than winning—clear indications the enemy is gaining strength. In any case, after seizing enemy property, transition to a defensive posture upon culmination.

Exploitation seeks to gain property from a retreating enemy force. Destruction of the enemy force is not an exploitation goal. As such, the exploitation must have a clear idea of (1) what territory or facilities to seize, (2) what each team's role is in the exploitation, and (3) what conditions or signals will indicate that the current mission will transition into exploitation.

Exploitation conduct is very similar in organization and conduct to the MTC. However, whereas the MTC is dedicated to a given axis of advance or targets the enemy force, the exploitation seeks a specific objective at a given geographical location. This means bypassing the enemy is not only acceptable, but in most cases it is desirable!

As a last note, a commander must look for signs of culmination. If the objective cannot be seized and held, the expenditure of good troops would be a complete waste. Furthermore, your gains from the previous operation may also be compromised. Do not wear your force too thin!

PURSUIT

The attack, MTC, and even defense must be prepared to capitalize on their tactical success by achieving further tactical victory and operational gains. The pursuit is a follow-up form of attack, or counterattack, when conducted from a defense. Like exploitation, the pursuit is *not* a primary attack. Therefore, it must be planned as a branch or a sequel of other operations. The primary operation must be prepared to transition into a pursuit at an appropriate time.

The pursuit makes use of the "hammer and anvil" tactic to conclusively engage the enemy. Typically, a vanguard or reserve force will envelop the enemy from a flank as a shaping operation, while the main body of the pursuit presses the enemy front as a decisive operation.

Why Use This Tactic?

The pursuit differs from exploitation because the pursuit has the specific goal of destroying or capturing the entire enemy force.

In order for you to pursue, the enemy must be in full retreat. That is why the pursuit is a follow-up attack. It depends on the success of a previous operation in sending the enemy into retreat. With the enemy retreating along their former lines of advance, several important phenomena are taking place that make the retreating enemy ripe for destruction—loss of formation, loss of coordination, and fleeing through escape routes.

Loss of Formation

Essentially there are two combat postures—offensive and defensive. Retreat is not a combat posture. Indeed, there are organized, well-disciplined withdrawals. Nonetheless, there is no "run away" formation in doctrine, regardless of how bravely you flee. When a retreating enemy is taking fire, the enemy is forced to assume a combat formation or continue to flee. Neither case is very desirable.

Forming into a combat formation while under fire is daunting at best and disastrous at worst! Fleeing under fire is simply an admission that we've degenerated into a "save yourself" state of mind. The normal succession of events compels the enemy's formation to take the shape of a long, vulnerable line as it retreats.

Loss of Coordination

Retreating is rarely ever planned as a branch or sequel to combat operations. Why is that significant? Because it means a well-coordinated retreat is as rare as rocking-horse poop. If the retreating enemy—having lost the formation of its combat posture—cannot communicate and coordinate

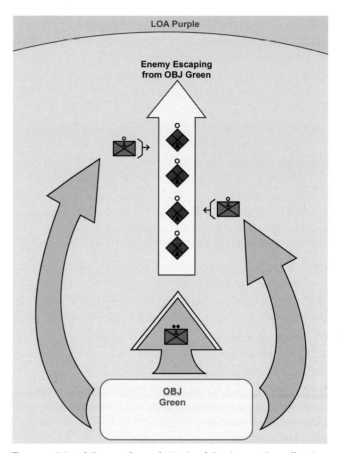

The pursuit is a follow-up form of attack—following another offensive action. Small teams deploy forward to envelop and fix the enemy in their escape route. The suppressed enemy cannot coordinate a defense, and the main force defeats them in detail.

its combat power, it becomes increasingly likely that each subordinate unit, team, and individual can be easily *isolated*.

Once the enemy troops are isolated from the support of their companions, a well-coordinated pursuit can quickly overwhelm and destroy these teams.

Fleeing via Escape Routes

The enemy spent a great deal of time identifying a suitable avenue of approach to conduct their operations. Unless they were absolutely brain-dead when conducting this task, they looked for the same things the friendly patrol looked for in an avenue of approach—cover and concealment. Yes, there are other considerations as well. Ease of movement is a consideration, but even this consideration makes concessions to the need for cover and concealment.

What all of this means is the enemy's avenue of approach—and, therefore, their line of retreat—likely makes use of low points in the terrain and plenty of bushy trees and such. These are great places to move troops and not be seen by the enemy. These are also natural "choke points"—death traps in the event of attack while moving through them!

So, the trick to an effective pursuit is to quickly mobilize either a vanguard or reserve as an enveloping force. This force moves either left or right at a high rate of speed and aggressively engages the retreating enemy in these choke points.

The idea isn't necessarily for the enveloping force to *destroy* the enemy in the choke point—unless the enemy attempts to flee. Instead, the enveloping force attempts to compel the enemy to assume a combat posture and form a hasty but isolated defense. That's because after the enveloping force finds and fixes the enemy in their avenue of retreat, the main force of this pursuit will finish off the small, isolated enemy. The enveloping force acts as the anvil, and the main force acts as the large hammer. The enemy is crushed in between.

This sequence is repeated in order to destroy as much of the enemy force as possible. It's a classic case of "Find 'em, fix 'em, finish 'em." That is the *main effort* of a pursuit—to close with the enemy force and kill or capture them all.

Form the Team

Obviously, this takes a great deal of coordination. It also requires a very fast enveloping force. The transition from any combat operation into a pursuit is not easy. The good news is that there are really only two teams to create—the enveloping force and the main force.

Typically, the enveloping force will be made up of a smaller team from the previous mission. From the attack, the relatively small reserve force is ideal for transitioning to an enveloping force. In this case, the main force and any vanguards of the attack would retain their status as a main force in the pursuit.

From an MTC, the relatively small vanguard force would transition to the enveloping force. The reserve—which makes up a major portion of the main body in an MTC—would become the main force of the pursuit.

From a defense, this is a bit trickier. If you had a good reason for taking a defensive posture, you probably don't want to abandon the defense to pursue the enemy. On the other hand, if you have absolutely no need to continue that defense, charge! In such a case, the defense's reserve force becomes the enveloping force, and the defensive line transitions into the main force of the pursuit.

Now, if the defense must continue to defend, the defensive line *may not* leave the defensive position! That's very important. So, the best the defense could do is dispatch the reserve force and envelop the enemy to catch them in their lines of retreat. In this case, there is no anvil—just a hammer. (Do the best you can.)

Commanders should position themselves with the main force. Very rarely would they travel with the enveloping force, since they need to direct the main-force attack.

Additionally, the enveloping force may be formed as a single team or break into two or more teams. The reason for breaking into two or more teams would be that this allows the enveloping force to fix *multiple*, isolated enemy teams

The pursuit seeks to find, fix, and finish a fleeing enemy force. An enveloping force moves quickly forward along a parallel route of the escaping enemy. The enveloping force makes contact, fixing pockets of the enemy in their escape routes.

With the enemy fixed in their escape route, the main body is called forward and moves in a direct path toward the pinned enemy. If possible, indirect fire is also employed to disrupt the enemy and keep them from coordinating an effective defense or counterattack.

along their routes of retreat. In turn, that allows a greater probability that the pursuit will succeed in destroying as much of the enemy force as possible.

Special Preparations

Preparing the battlefield is a bit difficult, since the pursuit is a follow-up attack. Admittedly, the previous mission gets the lion's share of the planning and preparation. Still, there are certain conditions that need to be considered as branches and sequels of the previous mission. Since the pursuit is a viable option after any successful tactical engagement, we'll take a moment to outline those conditions that make a pursuit feasible.

First and foremost, the bad guys *must be retreating!* It does little good to "plan the complete destruction" of the enemy while that enemy is quite comfortably sitting in his defensive position glaring down the barrel of his machine. They're not exactly vulnerable at that moment. Worse yet, plans for the most glorious pursuit are just about useless when the enemy is attacking.

A second and equally important condition is to have some knowledge of the avenues of advance—and, therefore, retreat—behind the enemy's position. Sure, the patrol could just take a stab at it—sort of a "shot in the dark." But when transitioning into a pursuit operation, it would be immensely beneficial for the enveloping force commander to know *exactly* where to go. Otherwise, the enveloping force is running around blind, desperately seeking out the enemy. Even if he does manage to find the enemy in a choke position in a timely manner, it is doubtful that he will be able to communicate his location accurately to the main force.

By the Numbers!

Because pursuit is planned as a branch or a sequel, it is virtually impossible to detail the execution, since so much depends on the status of the enemy forces after the primary operation concludes. However, pursuit has the intended goal of destroying or capturing the enemy force. And, as noted, the exact location of the enemy will not become clear until the first operation has achieved its objectives.

1. The commander and subordinate leaders must know where the enemy is located. A fixing force—typically the reserve of any combat operation—must move deeply into enemy territory to identify the enemy's routes of escape and relay this information back to the main force. The fixing force will trap the enemy in individual pockets within the escape routes to prevent the enemy from coordinating with adjacent enemy units. The main force will maneuver up to and destroy the trapped enemy. Then the process repeats in order to trap and destroy as many enemy troops as possible.

2. The pursuit is focused on the destruction of the enemy force. So bypass any terrain or facilities that do not present a threat to rear or flanks. Do not leave an enemy force behind capable of delaying either the fixing force or main force.

3. Finally, the commander must look for signs of culmination. Culmination, of course, means that the mission is coming to a reasonable conclusion. Remember, as you pursue the enemy, they are falling back on their own resources. Namely, they are falling back to designated rally points, which theoretically offer them defensive positions. If you run your troops to exhaustion and/or very small numbers, the enemy will likely counterattack. Be careful. Know when to quit.

The main body must move quickly and aggressively while the enveloping force still has the enemy pinned. The main body attacks and destroys the first pocket of the enemy. The enveloping force then fixes the next pocket, and the process continues until culmination.

CHAPTER 8
SPECIAL OPERATIONS

RECONNAISSANCE

A commander needs to know what lies ahead of the friendly force before, during, and after an engagement. The reconnaissance team provides the commander with eyes and ears. Recon is absolutely essential for situational awareness. Without it, he simply cannot know how to respond, and every course of action becomes a wild guess.

In spite of all the wonderful tools for conducting surveillance, the task of recon is a human endeavor. That means boots on the ground.

The recon team must not be discovered! Get the information, and get away free!

This will come as a surprise to many young troops, but Hollywood lied. Recon teams do not kill the enemy in knife fights or with silenced weapons. Nor do they booby-trap the objective or anywhere near the objective. Why? It's simple. If you let the enemy know you've discovered their secrets, they'll simply change their secrets, and all the work will be for nothing.

So, talk of "contact" does not necessarily mean engaging the enemy in a firefight. For reconnaissance, "contact" means to observe the enemy, develop the situation, and pass back the pertinent information the commander needs to make sound tactical decisions. The commander will employ his intelligence, surveillance, and reconnaissance (ISR) assets as either a "recon push" or "recon pull."

Recon push means, prior to a battle, the commander identifies one or more named areas of interest (NAI) for recon. In this manner, the recon team pushes toward an objective within the area of operation and develops the situation for the commander.

Recon pull means, during a battle, the commander identifies an enemy objective for one or more recon teams. In this manner, each recon team has significant latitude of movement throughout the AO to gain contact with the enemy, develop the situation, and pull the main force—altering the direction of advance to engage the enemy.

Reconnaissance, in all its forms, is a process of gathering information to help the commander shape his understanding of the battlespace. Reconnaissance uses many techniques and technologies to collect this information, but it is still largely a human endeavor.

Finally, there are four types of reconnaissance: area, zone, route, and reconnaissance in force.

Form the Team

Recon teams necessarily maintain freedom of maneuver. After all, if the recon team is committed to a battle, it would be very difficult to develop the situation and pass information back to the commander. Paradoxically, this also means recon teams must present *some* level of physical danger to the enemy. Otherwise, if the recon team is discovered, how can the team break contact? If they cannot break contact, they cannot maintain freedom of maneuver.

It's a bit of a circular argument. The practical solution is to organize the recon team with just enough troops—not too many and not too few. Too many troops may mean the recon team will move slowly and be quickly discovered. Too few troops may mean the recon team does not present a physical danger to the enemy force and may be easily suppressed and destroyed. The same is true with the recon team's armament. The recon team should carry enough armament to break contact but not so heavy a load that mobility is compromised.

In this way, a recon team presents as small a footprint as possible, yet still possesses enough combat power to be a threat if necessary. But how many troops is that? Well, that's a good question, and like all "good questions," I don't have the magic answer. It depends a great deal on the specifics of the mission.

Area Reconnaissance

For fans of military trivia, years ago, the area recon was called the "point recon." The area recon has the objective of obtaining detailed information on an identified terrain feature, man-made feature, or enemy force within a specified area. This area is much smaller in terms of space than the objectives for the other forms of recon and, thereby, allows for a much smaller recon team.

Zone Reconnaissance

A zone recon collects detailed information of the terrain, obstacles, routes, and enemy forces within a specified zone designated by boundaries on a map. The zone recon covers a much larger physical space than an area recon and requires considerable time to conduct. Necessarily, this will require a much larger recon force that will break into multiple recon teams in order to cover that greater physical space.

Route Reconnaissance

A route recon collects information along a specified line of communication (LOC) or direction of advance, such as a road, railroad, waterway, or simply an identified avenue of approach through difficult terrain. Of course, the required information includes road conditions, obstacles, bridges, enemy activity, and civilian traffic, but it also includes terrain considerations like natural choke points where the enemy might impose a threat along the route. The size of the recon team depends greatly on the size, length, and potential enemy threat already positioned along the route. In some cases, it takes a full platoon. In other cases, the route recon team can be as small as an area recon team.

Reconnaissance in Force

A recon in force is an intentional effort to engage the enemy and develop the situation once contact is made. This is done when there is little information regarding the enemy's location, disposition, or capabilities. This is a legitimate form of reconnaissance for larger-echelon military units, however, at the tactical level this is more commonly called the movement to contact (MTC). Please refer to the chapter on MTC for considerations of organization, preparation, and execution.

Special Preparations

The recon team develops specific information regarding the battlespace. There is very little preparation of the battlespace, with the exception of maneuver control measures marked on a map.

Maneuver control measures restrict the recon team's movement to the AO and partition the AO into phase lines so higher command can monitor the patrol's progress. Obviously, the less space the AO encompasses, the faster the recon team can achieve its stated goals.

First, the AO is identified on the map by drawing a continuous line around the entire area in the shape of a rectangle or square. This area is given a name and must include the start point and the objective. The AO is partitioned into multiple sections by drawing intersecting phase lines. Ideally, these phase lines run along prominent linear terrain features, such as a waterway, ridgeline, valley, or any man-made linear object. If no terrain features are available, the phase lines are drawn in an arbitrary overlay of the map. In any case, each phase line is given a name.

The very first phase line marks the near boundary of the AO, just behind the start point. That phase line is the line of departure (LD). The very last phase marks the farthest boundary of the AO, beyond the objective. That phase line is the limit of advance (LOA). Again, the LD and LOA are given names.

Finally, the commander will identify the objective (OBJ) and/or NAI on the map by marking them with a continuous line in the form of a circle or square. These, too, are given names.

The PL typically identifies any additional maneuver control measures. This might include a direction of advance, anticipated listening halts, en-route rally points (ERP), objective rally points (ORP), target reference points (TRP), and the like.

By the Numbers!

At this point, you know your specific recon mission and have received and developed maneuver control measures. Before delving into the execution of each type of reconnaissance, it's important to discuss the fundamentals of recon patrols. There are *seven rules* to remember.

Ensure continuous recon. Reconnaissance happens before, during, and after an engagement. Before the engagement, the recon team develops the commander's picture of the battlefield. During the engagement, the recon team lets the commander know if the plan is having its intended effect upon the enemy force. After the engagement, the recon team helps the commander to determine the enemy's next move.

Don't keep recon assets in reserve. Of course, do not run the recon team until it is exhausted. However, the recon team acts as the commander's eyes and ears forward. There is no reason to keep one ear or one eye in reserve! Manage recon assets to allow continuous reconnaissance, including a rest plan.

Orient on the objective. Don't just throw the recon team forward without a specified objective. Name the type of recon mission and name the objective within the AO. This helps the commander prioritize the recon assets and objectives, plus it gives focus to the recon team for the most economical use of time.

Report information rapidly and accurately. Over time, information loses value because, more often than not, the battlefield is rapidly changing. Recon teams give timely reports on exactly what they see (without exaggeration) and exactly what they do not see. A common mistake in reconnaissance is the failure to report when no enemy force or presence is detected. Failing to report does nothing for the commander. A report of negative activity gives the commander a better understanding of where the enemy is not located.

Retain freedom of maneuver. As stated earlier, a recon team that becomes engaged in a firefight with the enemy is fixed to a given location. Without the ability to maneuver, that recon team can only report what is to its immediate front and has become no more useful in developing the battlefield picture than any other line unit.

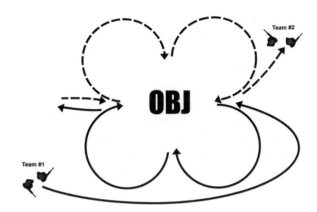

The clock method uses two teams to save time when tasked with an area recon. Team #1 moves to the twelve o'clock position (far side) of the objective, while Team #2 moves to recon from the six o'clock position (near side). Team #1 then moves to three o'clock, while Team #2 moves to nine o'clock. This affords multiple perspectives of the objective while minimizing the possibility of the two recon teams bumping into each other. That could be very dangerous.

Gain and maintain contact. Recon teams seek to gain contact with the enemy. More often than not, the recon team uses a combination of stealth and surveillance to maintain contact with the enemy. The recon team maintains contact with the enemy until the commander orders them to withdraw. The recon patrol leader may also break contact if the recon team is decisively engaged but then seeks to regain contact immediately.

Develop the situation rapidly. Once contact is gained, the recon team must quickly discern the threat. For an enemy force, that means identifying the enemy's approximate size of force, activity, direction of movement, and possibly disposition and capabilities. When evaluating an enemy obstacle, the recon team must discern the type of obstacle, the extent of the obstacle, and whether or not enemy fire covers it. Often, enemy obstacles tell the commander a fair amount of information regarding the capabilities and even location of the enemy force.

Area Reconnaissance

1. Upon occupying the ORP, the PL confirms the location of the recon objective. All special equipment is prepared for use, and plans are finalized. The PL issues contingency plans to the recon team(s) and to the security team left to defend the ORP.

2. The PL moves to the release point and dispatches the recon team(s) to approach the objective. Typically, the PL moves back to the ORP or may opt to accompany one of

the recon teams if troops are limited. This decision is made in the planning phase of the mission.

3a. **Single Team Method:** Using the clock method, the recon team approaches the recon objective from its closest point. This point now becomes the six o'clock position of the objective. The recon team will observe the enemy force, activity, and obstacles using stealth.

4a. The recon team records all pertinent information:
- A sketch of their vantage point, including terrain and enemy structures;
- An exact number of enemy personnel sighted;
- A descriptive list of all equipment, uniforms, and markings;
- The time of guard shift, eating, and sleeping shift rotations; and
- The direction, time, and size of any patrols coming or going from the area.

5a. The recon team then withdraws and maneuvers to the approximate nine o'clock position. The recon team repeats their observation and recording activities. The recon team continues to the twelve o'clock position and then the three o'clock position, obtaining information from all four vantage points if possible. At a minimum, the recon team must observe the targeted area from two vantage points.

3b. **Double Team Method:** When the troops are available, the PL may choose to dispatch two recon teams to the objective. This speeds information gathering but also creates a very real danger of fratricide. To coordinate this so there is little chance of the two recon teams' actually making contact, the teams are assigned opposite vantage points.

4b. Both teams are dispatched together and proceed toward the closest point of the targeted area. Upon locating this six o'clock position, a designated recon team would then withdraw slightly and proceed to the approximate twelve o'clock position.

5b. Both recon teams record the same pertinent information as mentioned above. However, the recon team at the six o'clock position will proceed only to the nine o'clock position and return to the ORP. Likewise, the recon team at the twelve o'clock position will proceed only to the three o'clock vantage point and return to the ORP.

6. **Dissemination of Information:** Once the recon team(s) returns to the ORP, all information is immediately disseminated among every recon patrol member. If there is time, additional copies of the sketches and record lists should be made. This will increase the likelihood of the gathered information making it back to the commander if the patrol is ambushed en-route.

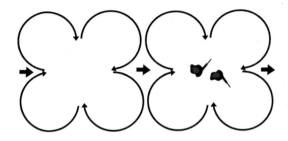

This method uses a series of en-route rally points to stop and dispatch the recon team. The team then moves to the next ERP. One recon team can cover only a very narrow zone. Zone recons tend to be time-consuming operations.

7. The recon team returns to the forward line of troops (FLOT) via a pre-designated route. Upon arrival, the PL reports directly to the commander.

Zone Reconnaissance

1. Upon occupying the ORP, the PL confirms the location of the recon objective. All special equipment is prepared for use, and plans are finalized. In this case, the ORP acts more like an assault. The patrol will not defend the ORP, nor will they return to the ORP. Every rule has its exception.

2. **Converging Route Method:** This method uses multiple recon teams that do *not* meet again until they rendezvous at the far side of the zone. This means a rally point is clearly established on an easily recognized terrain feature or landmark at the far side of the recon objective. Additionally, a near recognition signal ensures the fireteams do not mistakenly fire upon each other!

For larger zones, the converging route method uses multiple recon teams and, therefore, requires larger numbers of troops. En-route rally points (ERP) are established, and multiple recon teams move along terrain features until they meet up at the next ERP.

3. At the release point, the PL divides the patrol into the assigned recon teams. The PL must travel with one of these teams. The PL issues each recon team a contingency plan.

4. The recon teams depart the release point and move along parallel directions of advance through the specified zone. The recon teams stop at each phase line and NAI to conduct recons using the butterfly technique—which makes use of a series of designated, en-route rally points. The recon team pays particular attention to signs of enemy activity:

   • Fresh trash and cigarette butts indicate recent enemy activity
   • Boot prints and bent vegetation indicate the direction of enemy travel
   • The number of pressed vegetation spots at rest stops indicate the size of enemy patrols

   Also of great importance is the type of activity. For example, is the enemy running re-supply routes or ambush patrols? All enemy resources—outposts, water points, and obstacles like minefields—are thoroughly investigated.

5. Each time the recon teams reassemble in a rally point, information is disseminated and reported back to the PL, if possible. The PL, in turn, makes reports back to higher command.

6. The recon teams rendezvous at the far end of the objective, and the PL takes charge of all collected information, disseminates it to the patrol members, and issues another report to higher command.

Depending on the length of the route to be reconnoitered, the route recon may be conducted with great stealth, or it may be conducted with great mobility. In either case, the effort is still to gather intelligence on the route—its vulnerabilities and conditions.

7. The patrol moves back to the FLOT via an alternative route. It is generally not a good idea to return using the same route as the reconnaissance. If the enemy observed your movement, this COA carries the possibility of an enemy ambush. Upon arrival, the PL reports directly to the commander.

Route Reconnaissance

1. In the case of route recon, the patrol typically begins from the assembly area (AA), and the start point serves in the same manner as a release point. During a route recon, a highly mobile reserve force may follow a safe distance behind the recon team. In such cases, the PL issues a contingency plan for both the recon team and the reserve force.

2. The patrol moves along a designated direction of advance or LOC. At each phase line and NAI, the recon team conducts a security halt for the entire patrol, including the reserve force. This security halt becomes an ERP. From the ERP, the recon team gathers information using the butterfly technique.

3. The distance each recon team will travel out from the route depends greatly on the visibility of the terrain and/or the size of the obstacle. The recon team gathers all information regarding road conditions, obstacles, bridges, enemy activity, civilian traffic, and natural choke points along parallel terrain where the enemy might impose a threat.

4. Upon returning to the security halt, each recon team disseminates information among the patrol members. A written record is kept to log all information, and the PL will report to higher command after each rendezvous back at the ERP.

5. The recon patrol continues to the next phase line or NAI, and the entire process repeats itself until the patrol has adequately navigated the entire route. At that time, the PL moves the recon patrol back to the FLOT, or the patrol may be tasked to another mission. In either case, the PL must make a full report to higher command.

   The principles of *M*ission, *E*nemy, *T*errain and weather, *T*ime available, *T*roops available, *C*ivilians on the battlefield (METT-TC) dictate the reconnaissance effort. Though each principal consideration is important, time is critical in shaping the amount of stealth:

   Unlimited time + great detail needed means that considerable stealth is required.

   Limited time + little detail needed means that considerable speed is required.

Which to use? This is the art of tactics. The time a commander needs to develop a carefully considered COA gives the enemy plenty of preparation time. In such a case, it is imperative not to allow the enemy to know ISR assets are observing them. Get the information, and get away free!

On the other hand, if an objective can be seized today with acceptable casualties, it is possible that same objective will be far more costly tomorrow. In such cases where actions are pressed for time, it makes very little difference whether the enemy is aware of the activity because the unit achieves surprise through mobility.

AMBUSH!

Oh, yes! The ambush is where light infantry earn their paychecks. Personally, it is my favorite tactic, and I've argued for years to give this tactic its due—a lesson that needs an entire week dedicated to it. Obviously, no one ever gave me that much time to teach this lesson, but I'm sticking to my guns. It is critical to learn to ambush with great proficiency in daytime, nighttime, and all types of terrain and weather. The immediate and long-term effects of a well-executed ambush are devastating! A campaign of intense ambushes pays off at the tactical level, the operational level, and even the strategic level.

I could literally write a thesis on the ambush—and one day, I just might. However, I'll spare you that heavy reading for now. In the meantime, it's important to recognize many different ambush classifications.

The **point ambush** is the traditional ambush. The point ambush is executed by a single team, camouflaged along a high-speed avenue of approach like a road, footpath, or creek. This chapter emphasizes the point ambush almost exclusively.

The **area ambush** is simply a networked series of point ambushes, executed by multiple teams in a given area of operation (AO). The effort is to hit multiple targets simultaneously or almost simultaneously. Special care is given to the direction of fire to avoid fratricide against another ambush team and to seal the enemy's routes of escape—to hit a single target with two or even three ambushes in sequence.

You will also commonly hear the terms **hasty ambush** and **deliberate ambush**. This is to discern the hasty ambush—a battle drill—from a deliberately planned and executed ambush. The deliberate ambush is a tactic.

Now, of the many different classifications and methodologies, I argue the most important classification is to distinguish between **near ambush** and **far ambush**. Consider these two variations much more carefully when planning a deliberate point ambush.

Why Use This Tactic?

The intent of any ambush is to kill enemy troops and destroy enemy equipment. How and to what extent determines the difference between near ambush or far ambush.

Near Ambush

The near ambush has the expressed intent of absolutely destroying the target. This often requires an assaulting force to literally overrun the target after the initial volley of fire has inflicted tremendous damage, *destroying everything!*

To overwhelm the target, get as close as possible to the enemy. This close proximity also means outnumbering the enemy target is a MUST! Never, never, ever use a near ambush on an enemy force larger than your patrol.

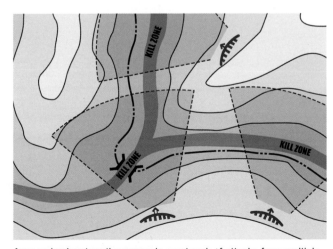

Area ambushes trap the enemy in a network of attacks from multiple concealed positions. These ambushes are carefully oriented to avoid "friendly fire." Often, this means taking advantage of terrain that protects other ambush teams in the immediate vicinity.

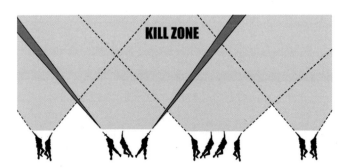

The near ambush has the express intent of overwhelming and destroying the enemy force. For this reason, the near ambush masses close to the kill zone and requires careful fire coordination. The linear method offers the greatest simplicity.

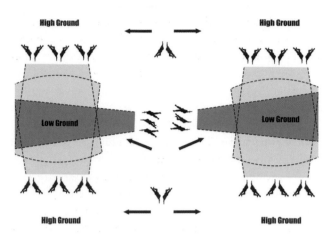

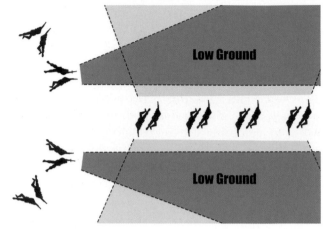

The "H" method uses considerable distance between the ambush patrol and the kill zone by occupying the valley's high ground. Longer distances also allow more elaborate coordination of fire. Support teams in the middle stop the enemy advance.

The "T" method is commonly used for near ambushes along a spur when uncertain which side of the spur the enemy is traveling. Buddy teams positioned on top of the spur face opposite directions to cover both possible avenues of approach.

Far Ambush

The far ambush only intends to injure and/or delay the target. This rarely ever calls for an assaulting force, since complete enemy destruction is not the goal. The far ambush is simply *harassment*.

A far ambush team can engage an enemy patrol of any size or type. It does not matter if the enemy force is larger because it utilizes significant distance, natural terrain obstacles, and established routes of withdrawal. That allows the ambush patrol to escape before the enemy has time to organize an effective counterattack.

Form the Team

An ambush patrol is broken into multiple teams, each with a very specific set of responsibilities. The team must be assigned a leader. The team must also work together, at least during the rehearsals prior to the mission. This lets members of the patrol understand their roles within that specific team and shows how their team fits into the bigger picture.

The ambush requires special equipment for each assigned team. This equipment should be available for the rehearsal as well to ensure everything functions according to the execution plan. Trust me, it's no fun discovering a communication device doesn't work when smack in middle of an ambush firefight!

Near Ambush

The near ambush breaks into three teams—the security team, the support team, and the assault team. Each team has

a specific set of duties, and the security and assault teams break down into further specialty teams.

The **security team** is responsible for the ambush's left, right, and sometimes rear security. As is often the case, the security team is also assigned to specific security details while the ambush patrol maneuvers to and from the intended ambush site. Additionally, a security team will be placed in an overwatch position after the leader's recon confirms the

The near ambush is broken into three teams—security, support, and assault. The security team is typically broken down further into a left, right, and sometimes rear security team. In this linear-shaped ambush, the teams are arranged accordingly.

exact site of the ambush. This security team will remain at the overwatch position while the patrol leader returns to the objective rally point (ORP) and brings the remainder of the ambush patrol forward.

The security team leader will take a position with the right or left security team. In the event a "rear security team" is required at the release point, the security team leader will stay at that position.

The **support team** is responsible for delivering effective, heavy-weapon fire against the enemy. The support team *rarely* ever breaks into separate teams but is positioned in the ambush formation to deliver accurate fire on the entire kill zone. The support team typically has machine gunners, grenadiers, and marksmen.

The **assault team** is responsible for augmenting the fire of the support team against the enemy during the initial volley. This act significantly impacts the target physically and also adds to the psychological shock of the ambush's violence of action. If a signal is given to sweep the kill zone after the initial volley of fire, the assault team must move forward to attack any surviving enemy in or around the kill zone.

The assault team also breaks into specialty teams. Those teams almost always include an "enemy prisoners of war (EPW) search team" to look for priority intelligence requirements (PIR)—such as enemy maps, orders, radio frequencies, and the like—and an "aid and litter" team to evacuate any friendly casualties. Additional specialty teams include a "demo team" to destroy or booby-trap enemy weapons and equipment, or a "grab team" to take EPW.

As a general rule, the ambush patrol leader takes a position with the support team in order to better initiate and coordinate the fire of the ambush. This is just a guideline, and the patrol leader may determine where best to control the ambush.

Far Ambush

The far ambush breaks into only two teams—the security team and the support team. However, these teams may be spread out over large distances and assume very specific responsibilities.

The **security team**, in a very similar manner to the near ambush, assumes responsibility for the far left and right sides of the formation. There is also a greater need for a rear security team to protect the multiple teams as they maneuver into their escape routes.

Also, the security team is responsible for security details as the ambush patrol moves to and from the ambush site. Again, the security team responsibilities are almost identical, regardless of whether it is a near or far ambush. The major difference for the security team is that the far ambush requires the security teams to be very far apart—often operating without visibility of each other. This takes considerable coordination because the security teams must protect the ambush force and ensure there is no friendly fire.

The **support team** is, again, responsible for delivering effective fire against the enemy. However, in the far ambush, the support team is *often* broken into separate teams in order to deliver accurate fire to the entire kill zone. The support team typically has machine gunners, grenadiers, and marksmen. Depending on the type of target, the support team for a far ambush may also include rocket launchers, combat engineers, and even mortar crews.

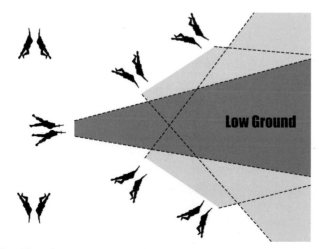

The "V" method is commonly used when conducting near ambushes along a single draw of a ridge. By occupying the high ground and directing fire downward, this method is extremely effective and safe in its simplicity.

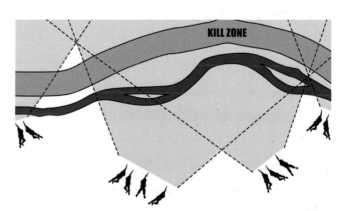

The far ambush keeps considerable distance between the ambush patrol and the enemy in the kill zone. Note, the creek is between the ambush team and the kill zone to offer protection from counterattack. The "L" method is common for the far ambush.

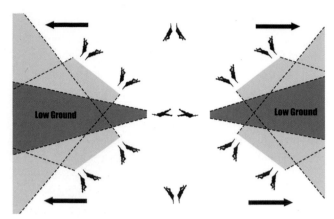

The "X" method, as well as a close variation known as the "Z" method, is an excellent choice when the enemy is known to be using a set of draws along a ridgeline for movement. This allows the ambush team to cover both avenues of approach by controlling the high ground in between. Both the "X" and the "Z" make use of two "V" ambush formations placed essentially back-to-back.

Special Preparations

Before the patrol goes running around the landscape searching for bad guys to ambush, a little preparation is required. At a minimum, intelligence from a previous reconnaissance effort must identify probable enemy activity to ambush. Additionally, using at least a map, it must identify a likely location for the ambush. Then, it must plan the direction of ambush patrol fire so as not to inflict casualties upon other friendly positions in the immediate area.

The decision to employ near or far ambushes depends on battlefield METT-TC. While all these considerations must be assessed, the size and type of the enemy target and the number of friendly troops determine selection of near or far ambush.

Near Ambush

Physically speaking, a near ambush is *close enough for the assault team to rush across*. In most types of terrain and vegetation, that means hand-grenade range—thirty-five meters. But remember, as the density of vegetation increases, the ability to rush forward decreases. In thick vegetation like a jungle, a near ambush may need to be employed as close as ten meters from the kill zone. Conversely, in wide-open terrain, a near ambush could be forty or even fifty meters from the kill zone.

The near ambush destroys the enemy target. It is preferred to have the patrol outnumber the enemy 2:1. If more evenly matched, that is acceptable. However, *never* employ a near ambush against a target numerically superior to the patrol. To achieve numerical superiority, know the approximate size of enemy patrols.

Finally, in preparing a near ambush, *employ obstacles on the far side of the kill zone*. The ambush intends to destroy the enemy target and does not want them escaping easily. These can be natural obstacles, such as the foot of a steep hill, a cliff, a large body of water, or a wide-open field that exposes the enemy troops as they run away. These can also be man-made obstacles, such as anti-personnel mines or well-camouflaged wire obstacles. The best technique employs multiple obstacles of both types.

Far Ambush

Physically speaking, a far ambush is *too far to rush across*. In almost all terrain, that includes distances significantly greater than thirty-five meters. Admittedly, within the most densely vegetated environments, an ambush at fifty or even forty meters might be considered a far ambush. But typically, far ambushes make use of distances of seventy meters up to seven hundred meters from the kill zone.

The far ambush is used to harass, injure, or delay the target. Due to the significant distances, there is no need to outnumber the enemy target. However, in order to effectively inflict damage, it will be beneficial to have some identification of the target. For example, is the target simply a supply convoy, or is it a combat patrol? Does the enemy employ armored vehicles, thin-skinned vehicles, or only foot patrols?

Last, in preparing a far ambush, *employ obstacles on the near side of the kill zone* and carefully *plan and identify escape routes* to allow your ambush patrol time to escape before the enemy target recovers and counterattacks after the initial volley of fire. The obstacles in between the ambush patrol and the enemy—whether man-made or naturally occurring—serve to slow the enemy counterattack. The clearly identified escape routes speed escape and simplify coordination.

By the Numbers!

Let's get one thing straight, right from the beginning. A high volume of fire in the ambush has more shock value than accurate fire. Violence of action is the key to a successful ambush. To achieve this, the ambush patrol must shoot in unison. When that first shot of initiating fire cracks in the air, *everyone will shoot!* It must sound like deafening thunder! It should sound like a firing squad. In effect, it *is* a firing squad.

The alternative is disaster. If every weapon on the ambush does not instantaneously join the opening shot—if the patrol members attempt to find a suitable target, slowly increasing the rate of fire—the ambush will die! The enemy will have plenty of time to react. They will rush into the ambush and fight viciously for their lives.

Do not hesitate on an ambush! Wait for the initiating shot, and empty your magazine!

Near Ambush

The near ambush should *shock* and *destroy* the target. The patrol must shoot rapidly when they hear the initial shot of the ambush. Be close enough to the enemy to smell them. Competition marksman skills aren't needed here.

1. The patrol will occupy an ORP either one terrain feature or approximately three hundred meters away from the intended ambush site. The PL will assemble the leader's recon team and issue a five-point contingency plan to the APL prior to leaving on the recon. At a minimum, the leader's recon will include the PL, a two-man security team, and either the assault team leader or the support team leader—typically the team he will *not* accompany.

2. At the designated ambush site, the PL ensures that it is an appropriate terrain by using the considerations of *O*bservation, *C*over and concealment, *O*bstacles, *K*ey terrain, and *A*venues of approach (OCOKA). He does this without contaminating the kill zone—meaning he shouldn't actually walk through or onto the kill zone but should move around

After the initial volley of fire, the commander may give the signal for the assault team to attack across the kill zone. The support team and security teams must first lift or shift their fire to prevent "friendly fire" against the assault team.

to view it from the far right, from the far left, and from the middle of the ambush formation. If the terrain is not suitable for a near ambush, the PL chooses an appropriate site nearby.

3. The PL then posts the two-man security team far back, where they are easily concealed but can still view the kill zone. This post later becomes the release point. The security team sits back-to-back, with one man facing the kill zone and the other facing back toward the ORP. The PL will leave these men with a five-point contingency plan and return to the ORP. The security team must monitor all enemy activity and report this to the PL upon his return. It will be critical to know if the enemy has stopped on or near the ambush site.

4. After returning to the ORP, the PL coordinates any changes to the original plan with every member of the ambush patrol. Final preparations are conducted in the ORP, and the PL pulls together the patrol. The order of march will be the PL, security team, support team, and assault team. This is the exact order because the ambush goes into position using this sequence.

5. The PL leads the patrol to the security team at the release point. He links up the two-man security team with their security team leader. If the intended location of the left and right side security areas can be seen from the release point, the PL will have the security team leader place his teams into position. If the locations cannot be seen, the PL positions the left and right security teams, *taking the security team leader with him*.

6. Once the left and right security teams are in position, the PL returns to the release point and picks up the support team. He positions them into the formation, typically in front of the release point. The PL returns back to the release point and picks up the assault team. They, too, are placed in formation and typically assume the opposite (left or right) side of the support team.

7. With everyone in place, the PL takes his place as the leader of either the support or the assault team as determined in the operation order (OPORD). The PL conducts a communication system check, and then everyone settles down for a nice, long wait. Security stays at one hundred percent. No sleeping!

8. The ambush patrol continues to wait in position until:

- The PL gives the "end time" signal indicating the patrol must return
- The PL gives the "no fire" signal and allows a larger enemy force to pass
- The PL initiates the ambush

Specialty teams, such as the PIR Search Team, come from within the assault team. This is partly because the assault team tends to be the largest team on the ambush, but also because only one team maintains control over the kill zone at any given time.

9. The ambush patrol fires upon the kill zone only when:

- The PL initiates fire against the enemy in the kill zone
- The enemy fires upon the ambush patrol

Actions on the Objective

1. The actions on the objective will take no longer than *one minute to complete*. All members of the ambush patrol fire into the kill zone regardless of whether or not they see a specific target. The only exceptions could be security teams, who may not have a clear view of the kill zone.
2. The PL gives the signal to cease fire, to shift fire, or to lift fire. At this moment, the PL decides if it is reasonably safe for the assault team to move across the kill zone.
3. If the assault team is sent across the kill zone, it conducts the following actions in exactly this order:
   a. Sweep the kill zone online, being certain to double-tap all enemy
   b. Secure the far side of the kill zone
   c. Send the necessary specialty teams back into the kill zone to search for PIR, aid friendly casualties, or destroy enemy equipment
4. The assault team leader gives the thumbs-up signal to the PL, indicating the far side of the kill zone is secure, and the specialty teams have finished their tasks. The assault team secures the far side of the kill zone until the PL signals to fall back.
5. The PL gives the signal for the assault team to fall back through the release point to the ORP. The assault team does so without hesitation and doesn't wait for other teams.

6. The PL gives the signal for the support team to fall back through the release point to the ORP. The support team does this immediately.
7. Last, the PL will give the signal for the security team to fall back through the release point and move to the ORP. The PL will wait for the security team at the release point and move back to the ORP with this element. In this manner, the ambush has displaced in the exact reverse order from which it was emplaced.

Reconsolidate and Reorganize

1. The assault team is the first element to get back to the ORP. The assault team leader forms the ORP into a 360-degree security area and continues to shape the ORP until a senior leader replaces him. He also distributes ammunition and water as needed.
2. Everyone must be accounted for, and casualties must receive medical aid. This will continue until all elements and the PL have returned to the ORP. Once every member is accounted for, the PL will ask for a sensitive-equipment check. Each patrol member accounts for his assigned equipment by physically touching the item.
3. The PL will facilitate the dissemination of PIR to all members of the patrol. This is necessary because, should the patrol later become engaged and take casualties, the PIR must be relayed to higher command. If the PL is the only patrol member informed of the PIR, and the PL becomes a casualty, the effort of the patrol would be lost.
4. The designated route of return and plans to evacuate casualties and/or EPW will be followed in accordance with the OPORD. Continue the mission.

Far Ambush

The goal in the far ambush is to *inflict damage* upon an enemy patrol. There is no requirement to overrun the target. In fact, the patrol doesn't even have an assault team. It helps to think of the far ambush as a grandiose sniper mission. After all, if one sniper team is good, a half dozen or more is even better, right? Just throw in a machine-gun position or two, and that's impressive sniping power! If expecting armored vehicles, just add a few hunter-killer teams with rocket launchers. You can get as fancy or as simple as you want.

1. The PL assembles a team to conduct the leader's recon at an ORP an appropriate distance away from the intended ambush site. This team includes the PL and the entire security team. Prior to heading out on the recon, the PL leaves the support team leader with a five-point contingency plan.

2. The PL moves the recon team to the intended ambush site and posts the security team in a position that affords a complete view of the ambush site. Then, the PL and the security team leader move to the far left, far right, and middle to determine if the terrain is appropriate, to determine where to place the security and support teams, and to identify routes of escape. Furthermore, the kill zone must have some type of natural obstacle between the enemy and the ambush patrol to slow the enemy's counterattack. If no natural obstacle exists, then employ and camouflage a man-made obstacle. If the terrain is simply inappropriate for this mission, choose another location nearby.

3. The PL positions the entire security team toward the middle of the ambush line so they can view the kill zone. This becomes the release point. The PL leaves a five-point contingency plan with the security team leader and returns to the ORP.

4. The PL disseminates any changes to the original plan to all patrol members back at the ORP. Complete final preparations and form the support team. The support team may break into sub-teams to form the order of march according to the OPORD. The PL will link up the support teams with the security team.

5. At the release point, the PL releases each element to the team leader. The security team leader places his teams as directed. The support team leader places his teams, and the PL moves with whichever support team he decides will give him the best view of the kill zone and command of the elements.

6. With all elements in place, the PL conducts a communication systems check. The entire patrol waits in place for the ambush to initiate. In the far ambush, due to the distance between elements, the left or right side security will often be the first to see the enemy element. They inform the PL on enemy movement and estimated time of arrival.

7. It is unlikely the enemy will detect the ambush patrol in a far ambush mission. Still, the same rules apply to the far ambush that apply to the near ambush:

- The PL gives the "time" signal that indicates the patrol must return
- The PL gives the "no fire" signal and allows a large enemy team to pass
- The ambush initiates

8. The ambush patrol fires upon the kill zone only when:

- The PL initiates fire against the enemy in the kill zone, or
- The enemy fires upon the ambush patrol.

Actions on the Objective

1. The actions on the objective depend upon the enemy's ability to react. The far ambush continues until the enemy escapes the kill zone, the enemy begins a counterattack, or the PL is satisfied with the effect of the ambush. This may

The far ambush places high value on marksmanship skills. The support team is often broken into a series of sniper, machine-gun, and rocket teams firing into the kill zone from multiple, coordinated directions. This complicates the enemy response.

Escape routes are an important consideration for any ambush, but they are absolutely vital to the far ambush. Once the far ambush has achieved its effect, defilades, ravines, and draws are used as escape routes. Quit before the enemy is behind you!

take a minute or an hour. Do not fire *all* ammunition. The patrol still has to escape. And remember, the longer the patrol stays, the more vulnerable it becomes.

2. Upon the signal to cease fire, the support teams automatically withdraw to the ORP using the designated escape route. There is no need to pass through the release point. This will waste time due to the distance between elements.

3. The PL travels with one of the support teams. When he calculates that he has passed the release point, he signals the security team to withdraw. The security team leader rallies his team in a concealed area *behind* the release point to make certain to account for the entire team. Then the security team proceeds to the ORP.

Reconsolidate and Reorganize

1. The PL arrives back at the ORP and forms a 360-degree security area until all patrol members are assembled. Distribute ammunition and water as needed. Casualties receive medical aid.

2. Once every member is accounted for, the PL asks for a sensitive-equipment check. Patrol members count their assigned sensitive equipment (weapons, radios, night-vision devices, etc.) by physically touching the item.

3. Far ambushes also attempt to gain PIR, and all observations are quickly disseminated. The designated route of return and plans to evacuate casualties are conducted according to the OPORD. Continue the mission.

The ambush is perhaps the most effective light-infantry combat patrol. When conducted properly, it affects every level of warfare and significantly impacts the enemy's morale, logistics, and movement. To be successful, avoid the common mistakes of the ambush.

On the near ambush, the most common mistake is the failure to fire after the initial shot. A slow escalation of fire gives the enemy vital seconds to react. The most confusing scenario for the ambush patrol is when the enemy target moves into the kill zone, but instead of hearing an initiating shot, a weapon misfires. In this instance, *the misfire must be treated as the initiating shot*. If it isn't treated as such, the first shot will come from the enemy!

Another mistake may be that, after carefully planning a route of escape, the patrol stays too long. The targets of opportunity are usually rich in the far ambush, and the risk of personal injury is much less significant than the near ambush. This advantage creates overconfidence. However, the enemy is likely a larger force than the patrol. They will invariably determine position and counterattack. If

that happens, all the carefully planned escape routes are useless! It takes a cool head for the PL to know when the patrol has inflicted enough damage and when to withdraw. Remember, the far ambush doesn't seek to completely destroy the enemy but just to *inflict damage*.

SWARMING ATTACK

Like the raid and ambush, the swarming attack is a specialized form of attack. The swarming attack uses highly distributed forces converging at a single point to mass an attack against the enemy. That means you don't need total numerical superiority over your opponent, you only need numerical superiority *at the local point of engagement*.

Swarming attacks are well-suited for low-intensity conflicts. For this reason, the swarming attack is a common tactic within counterinsurgency (COIN) operations. It is used both by guerilla forces attempting to assert dominance over a regional conflict and by the host nation and/or international military forces that attempt to coerce such guerillas back to a peaceful diplomatic solution.

Why Use This Tactic?

The swarming attack seeks to destroy an enemy target through a series of pulsating, coordinated attacks from multiple directions. The effort is not necessarily to defeat the enemy in a single attack, but through a series of attacks that disorient and erode the enemy force.

There are two recognized methods for swarming attacks:
1. Massed swarming: The force begins as a massed unit and breaks apart to swarm against an identified target.

Swarming attacks are dispatched from either dispersed or massed locations. When massed, the swarming attack resembles bees coming out of a hive. When dispersed, the swarming attack resembles ants coming from multiple anthills onto a single target.

Highly desirable for the swarming attack are weapons that allow the swarming force to attack from significant distances—beyond the sight of the enemy—such as mortar and command-detonated mines. This aids in the effort to confuse and disorient the enemy.

2. Dispersed swarming: The force is geographically dispersed from the start of the mission and converges to attack once a target is identified.

Dispersed swarming is the more effective of the two methods because the attacking force never presents a massed target for the enemy to engage. However, dispersed swarming takes the greatest planning and coordinating efforts because the force is never co-located for the planning and rehearsal phase. Furthermore, while both methods for swarming attacks require considerable reliance upon the junior leader, the dispersed swarm method involves semi-autonomous teams. Dispersed swarming operations require advanced leadership competencies, or coordination and synchronization will not be achieved.

Dispersed swarming is typically reserved for military units larger than the platoon—at least at the company or battalion level. Platoons and squads more commonly make use of massed swarming. Admittedly, this decision is situation-dependent.

The swarming attack requires three characteristics for success:

- Elusiveness
- Standoff capability
- Situational awareness

Elusiveness can be achieved either through mobility or concealment. Standoff capability requires advanced communication and targeting systems coupled with long-range firepower. And situational awareness is achieved through an acute understanding of your Strengths, Weaknesses, Opportunities, and Threats (SWOT) versus the enemy's SWOT. Such an understanding takes into consideration the factors of METT-TC within the COE.

Form the Team

A platoon typically breaks down into three squads for a total of six fireteams. One fireteam should be held in reserve with the command team. All fireteams must be equipped with radios or cell phones for communication. The swarming attack requires:

- Autonomy
- Mobility
- Communication
- Synchronization

Autonomy. The swarming attack differs significantly from a conventional attack or MTC because the attacking force is dispersed along a much greater geographical area. This dispersing has two advantages. First, it does not offer the enemy a massed target to engage with mass-casualty-producing weapons. Second, it allows the swarming attack force to gather more human intelligence because the patrol is spread out over such a large area.

Admittedly, this type of formation goes against the massed, linear hierarchy of command mindset. That is why the swarming attack falls under the category of specialized forms of attack. Like the raid and the ambush, the swarming attack hits the enemy in an unpredictable space, time, and manner. The nature of such specialized attacks relies on the decentralized and independent operations of a small military force.

The swarming attack also relies on a well-communicated commander's intent. This is because the small-team leader will often find himself in a position in which the original plan is no longer feasible. In such situations, the philosophy of *Auftragstaktik* applies—the notion that the junior leader may make decisions that appear to be in direct conflict with the original order even though he is trying to achieve the commander's expressed goal for the mission. That is why the commander's intent is so critical for such specialized missions.

Decentralized and autonomous units require small-unit commanders who are capable and have the latitude to make their own decisions within the framework of the commander's intent. Yet, swarming forces must be constantly aware of the location and presence of friendly units—thus, the reliance upon communication and synchronization. Otherwise, swarming forces inadvertently attack one another.

Mobility. All things being equal, a small team travels faster than a large team. One car makes a cross-country trip faster than

Swarming attacks also use highly mobile resources as a form of elusiveness. When the resources are available, and the terrain is permissive, mobility is used to achieve surprise through a quick strike that withdraws in a pulsing action.

Swarming attacks use the most primitive and most advanced means of gaining situational awareness. Only when the enemy presence is known can their weaknesses be exploited. More often than not, swarming attacks are asymmetrical.

ten cars. Four troops walk through the jungle faster than forty troops. This is the essence of the swarming attack's mobility.

It's true, if your patrol has helicopter-lift capabilities, your swarming attack will be exponentially faster than the enemy's ability to respond. The same could be said for the enemy if they have some type of vehicle support. So, if that is the case, try to mitigate the enemy's advantage.

If the enemy has helicopters and your force does not, use the heavy canopy of the jungle to hide your movements. If the enemy has wheeled vehicles and your force does not, use the channeling effects of the city to expose the enemy's movements. If the enemy has tracked armored vehicles and your force does not, conduct operations in the steep mountains where tanks cannot pass.

In any case, for the swarming attack force, your teams will operate as small and highly mobile teams. They will adjust quickly to the changing battlefield and position themselves to your patrol's advantage.

Communication. Swarming attacks place great emphasis on communication and targeting technologies.

Technology has historically been a mixed bag. Technology dependence has produced as many battlefield failures as it has successes. Even when successful, technological advantages are always temporary. Still, technology can, in part, satisfy the need to locate the enemy.

Without adequate communication technology, synchronization between elements of a swarming attack takes place through line-of-sight communication, such as hand and arm signals and runners. These methods of communication are slow and likely will not produce the tempo necessary to defeat a modern, disciplined military.

Synchronization. Your swarming attack must *simultaneously* hit the enemy from multiple vantage points. After dispersing, you will regroup and reform into your separate teams and, again, simultaneously counterattack to achieve the pulsing effect.

Synchronization is achieved through:

- Established communication networks
- Coordinated zones of influence
- Pre-positioned supply caches
- Pre-positioned casualty evacuation points
- Standardized equipment and weapon systems
- Shared supplies within the swarming network

Special Preparations

One of the greatest challenges of the swarming attack is

Excellent communication is key to a synchronized attack. More often than not, the swarming force does not have enough combat power to eliminate the enemy in a single strike, and attacks must pulsate.

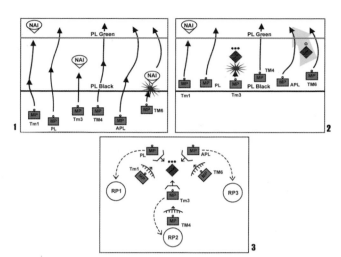

Swarming attacks function similar to a movement to contact (MTC) but without a main assault force held in reserve. Each small team is assigned a direction of attack and named areas of interest. Any identified enemy can be surrounded to take fire from three directions while baited ambushes are set.

to prevent friendly fire. This takes considerable planning and organization.

Your patrol forms into a massed swarming attack, since it is highly unlikely a platoon or squad would conduct a dispersed swarming attack. As such, you must utilize a map overlay to assign a parallel axis of movement for each fireteam. Typically, a platoon conducting a swarming attack divides the platoon's advance into five separate axes of movement—one per fireteam, with the last fireteam following in reserve with the command team. Five axes must be sketched into the platoon's advance.

The fireteams act independently. As such, radio communications are paramount in establishing situational awareness. Phase lines must be sketched onto the map overlay. These phase lines intersect each axis of movement at fairly regular patterns, and each fireteam leader must communicate his position when crossing each designated phase line.

Designate pre-determined rally points on the map overlay. These should include easy-to-locate terrain features naturally suited to defensive position. These rally points will be used to coordinate movements and halts and to act as an ORP from which to pulse the swarming attack.

Assign brevity codes for each of these organizational concerns—names for each fireteam's axis of movement, a name for each phase line, and names for each rally point. These codes are used to continue the swarming attack, change missions, or withdraw. Distribute brevity codes and radio frequencies to all members of the patrol.

By the Numbers!

Swarming attacks, like all battles, rely on the commander's ability to stack the force's strengths against the enemy's weaknesses. As with any tactic, the swarming attack will not work against all types of opponents in all situations.

The swarming attack seeks an asymmetric battle. When the enemy's defenses are strong, attack their patrols and disrupt their sleep patterns with attacks during the day and night. When the enemy's defenses are passive, attack along their lines and seek the path of least resistance. When the enemy sends out large patrols to conduct operations, attack the weakened defensive line once the larger patrols have departed.

Swarming is conceptually broken into four stages: locate, converge, attack, and disperse. The swarming attack must sustain a pulsing tempo. Swarming forces must be able to come together on target, disperse, and reform for a new pulse rapidly and with great stealth. It is critical that swarming forces converge and attack simultaneously!

1. **Locate:** The commander resides with a command team and directs the actions of the individual patrols using the maneuver control measures identified on the map. As a patrol comes into contact with the enemy, care must be taken to *avoid* an engagement! If the point patrol—that patrol with visual contact of the enemy—becomes engaged in a firefight, they cannot continue to develop the situation. That means the patrol fails in its responsibility to function as an Intelligence, Surveillance, and Reconnaissance (ISR) asset.

Furthermore, it is highly unlikely the tiny patrol will be able to effectively fix the enemy to any location. More likely, the massive enemy force will quickly destroy the patrol. If the patrol does become decisively engaged, they must break contact and seek a new vantage point to report on the enemy.

2. **Converge:** Once informed as to the enemy position, the commander must determine whether this is the high-priority target, a low-priority target, or a decoy. If the commander determines this to be a priority target, he will inform the other patrols to quickly converge on the target—using the maneuver control references—and mass the multiple patrols into an appropriate formation for an attack.

The Barbed Bull Horn (five points) formation uses multiple vantage points to conduct an attack by fire against the enemy position. Additionally, each of these vantage points serves as a "baited ambush" if the enemy gives chase.

3. **Attack:** The commander gives the order to attack, synchronizing the assaults. This disrupts the enemy because attack by fire comes from multiple directions. The enemy is confused about the direction of the primary attack. Since physical assaults occur only when it is to the patrol's advantage—against weakened targets of opportunity—the objective of the swarming force is not immediately apparent to the enemy force.

When the enemy takes offensive action against a swarming patrol, that patrol will yield their position and move through the supporting patrol's hasty ambush prepared kill zone.

No patrol leader should spend troops to defend ground!

In fact, it is desirable that the enemy force give pursuit and get lured into the waiting kill zone. Once the enemy becomes bogged down and loses forward momentum, the patrols must again take up multiple vantage points and attack by fire.

4. **Disperse:** The commander directs a hit-and-run style requiring these small teams to immediately fall back to designated positions. The commander and patrol leaders base the swarming attack pulsation on emergent dynamic—what the enemy is doing and where they are currently located.

As the attack continues, the commander must rally and rest individual patrols at locations he will designate using the maneuver control measures. The commander and patrol leaders must retain or regain visual contact between the pulsed attacks. Look for the enemy's strengths and weaknesses and play against their weaknesses.

5. The swarming attack will continue until the commander recognizes the signs of culmination, which may include the defeat or surrender of the entire enemy force. Conversely, it may mean the enemy has escaped detection, or that the patrols have exhausted troops, supplies, or ammunition, or that the enemy's actions have caused the patrol to lose the majority of the engagements. When he recognizes signs of culmination, the commander must direct the patrols to withdraw and transition to another form of combat operation.

Swarming operations are ideal for COIN operations. Guerillas must remain elusive, operating as small, highly mobile teams dispersed over a large area. Swarming forces physically cover a greater geographic area than the traditionally massed attack force and are more likely to pick up battlefield intelligence. A swarming network dispersed over a large area can perform frequent and random reconnaissance and can quickly react to suspected areas of enemy activity.

Swarming doctrine is not new. Alexander the Great had to contend with such swarming attacks by the Scythian horse archers. In fact, the principal characteristics of swarming doctrine are common to many other combat operations.

Many savvy readers have already noticed the swarming attack functions much like the reserve force in a mobile defense. While swarming attacks assume an offensive mode, the principal characteristics of the swarming attack and mobile defense do have remarkable similarities and compliment each other's tactical symmetry.

Elusiveness and situational awareness are essential to swarming attacks. History has shown that standoff weaponry is not as essential, though it is extremely desirable that the

Each patrol acts independently during swarming attacks, though their efforts are coordinated. Accordingly, small-unit leaders must be very well trained or experienced. The patrols move along assigned sectors using stealth to appear and disappear elusively.

swarming force may deliver a decisive blow with such weaponry. However, if the swarming attack's elusiveness or situational awareness is compromised, the attack is doomed to failure against a well-disciplined enemy.

Your patrol's communication systems are paramount to achieving situational awareness, as well as synchronization. Take extra care to prevent the communication system from being compromised. Likewise, the enemy's targeting systems present the biggest danger to your patrol's elusiveness. These targeting systems must be impaired or, better yet, destroyed.

RAID!

A successful raid is the hallmark tactic of Special Operational Forces and a crowning achievement for any infantry unit. No tactical maneuver requires a more advanced set of skills—intelligence-gathering through reconnaissance, brilliant planning, accurate rehearsals, and individual and team skill craft that is the envy of others. The moxie to pull off a precision raid is the stuff of history novels!

The raid is a specialized form of attack. Raiding patrols travel well into enemy territory. This means the raiding force can expect to be outnumbered, outgunned, and far from help. Any half-baked notion of Rambo-esque bravado spells certain failure. After all, if any bonehead could pull off a successful raid, it wouldn't be the hallmark tactic of the Special Operational Forces, would it?

Why Use This Tactic?

A raid is a surprise attack from a concealed position upon a stationary enemy target. Raids temporarily overwhelm enemy targets, usually deep within enemy territory.

There are many reasons to conduct raids. The patrol might be tasked to destroy key enemy equipment or facilities, temporarily seize key terrain, gather intelligence items, or liberate allied personnel. This may even include rescuing brothers in arms. While each of these missions differs from the next, they each entail a set of basic considerations.

Form the Team

In a very similar manner as the ambush force, the raiding force breaks down into three main elements: the security team, the support team, and the assault team.

The **security team** most commonly sets up to the left, right, and sometimes rear of the raiding party as the formation deployed around the objective. They carry rifles, light machine guns, anti-personnel mines, and possibly anti-armor capabilities to stave off reinforcing vehicles. Their

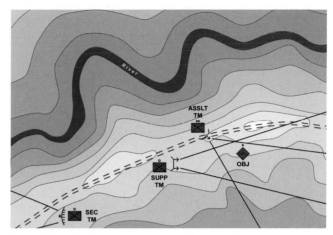

The raid has all of the same component teams as the ambush—security, support, and assault. The principal difference is that the raid is conducted on stationary targets, whereas, the ambush is used on moving targets. Thus, raids require greater stealth.

main purpose is to deter the enemy from reinforcing the objective and to seal the escape of any enemy.

The **support team** is commonly deployed center of the raiding formation so they have a clear view of the objective. They carry heavier mass-casualty-producing weapons, such as machine guns, grenade launchers, or missiles. This team is primarily responsible for the shock effect, as well as inflicting as many enemy casualties as possible.

The **assault team** is deployed as closely to the objective as stealth and coordinated fire support allow. They are lightly armed with rifles and carbines but may have special equipment. This team is responsible for the destruction, capture, or liberation of the target. Upon assaulting across the objective, they are also the most exposed and least armed element of the raid.

Raids also have sub-groups within the assault team. Examples of these specialty teams would include grab teams for abduction, prisoner search teams for intelligence requirements, aid and litter teams for wounded, demolition or explosive ordinance disposal (EOD) teams, and possibly even chemical, biological, radiological, and nuclear (CBRN) recovery teams.

Of course, you won't need all of these teams on a single raid unless you are a British 007 agent sent to save the world from a mad scientist whose nuclear bomb threatens a dastardly act of terrorism while a ravenously beautiful supermodel-turned-engineer has been bound and gagged within the blasting radius of this all-too-familiar Hollywood story of destruction! In that case, sure, use them all.

Special Preparations

The raid requires up-to-date information, which aids battle-space intelligence preparation (IPB). This translates into effective maneuver control measures, fire control measures, and a brilliant plan that makes ample use of stealth and timing. Rehearsals are an essential part of raid preparation.

The enemy will likely have good communications with reinforcements in the immediate vicinity, making the patrol vulnerable to counterattack. Severe time constraints exist from the moment the raid begins until the moment the patrol withdraws from the objective.

Obviously, a raid will be much more successful if the patrol has the element of surprise. To maximize this surprise, attack at a time when the enemy is least likely to expect an attack. Attack when visibility is limited and, if possible, from an unexpected avenue of approach, such as from seemingly impassable terrain. Know the terrain surrounding the objective very well.

The patrol leader leaves a two-man security team at the release point, ideally overlooking the objective. This security team must have a contingency plan. Then the patrol leader returns to the ORP to pick up the remainder of the patrol.

By the Numbers!

A raid's violence of action must cause a great deal of shock effect. A generous dose of firepower and tenacious attack stun and disorient the enemy. Do not underestimate the psychological effect of violence. If the enemy on the objective believe the patrol is actually much larger due to massed firepower and violence, they are less likely to stand and defend against the assaulting team. Furthermore, after the patrol has withdrawn from the objective, the enemy will pursue much less aggressively if they believe the patrol's numbers to be very large.

1. Once the objective rally point (ORP) is occupied and secured, the patrol leader (PL) conducts a leader's recon of the objective. At a minimum, the PL takes a two-man security team and the leader of the support or assault team—whichever one the PL will *not* be positioned with during the raid. Of course, it is generally considered a good idea to bring all three element leaders if possible.
2. The PL leaves a contingency plan with the assistant patrol leader (APL) in the ORP before departing. The leader's recon conducts a physical inspection of the objective, making certain everything is as planned. If not, the PL improvises any change to the plan . . . and since there will be no time or space for rehearsals, the option to change the plan should only be used in extreme circumstances.
3. The PL leaves a two-man security team with communication and a contingency plan. The security team is positioned to maintain constant observation of the objective to ensure that enemy reinforcements do not arrive and that the target doesn't leave. This spot will later

The patrol leader leaves the assistant patrol leader in the ORP with a security force. The raid patrol will drop all gear unnecessary for actions on the objective at the ORP. For this reason, the ORP needs to be secured until the patrol returns later.

The patrol leader moves the patrol forward to link up with the release point. From the release point, the patrol waits while the security teams carefully and quietly move to their assigned locations. Remember the enemy *is* on the objective!

become the release point. The PL and element leader(s) move back to the ORP.

4. The PL issues any changes to the plan in the ORP and finalizes all preparations. Picking up the rest of the patrol, the PL leads them out of the ORP and toward the release point in the following order:

- PL leads at point
- Security team
- Support team
- Assault team pulls up the drag

5. Upon reaching the release point, the PL checks with the on-site security team to make certain everything is okay. The PL then links the entire security team with the leader and gives them time to move into their designated positions. Unlike the ambush, the PL does NOT have the option of positioning each element. On a raid, the elements have all rehearsed exhaustively on where to go. Time must be allowed for each team member to stealthily position themselves. This requires some time and the use of communication devices.

6. The PL releases the support team next and may travel with them if he has not assigned himself to the assault team. The assault team takes position last and, due to the close proximity of their position to the objective, they must have ample time to move.

7. All elements wait for the signal to commence fire. This may be indicated by a fixed time or a designated signal, or the PL may issue the "No Fire" signal, in which case, the patrol withdraws.

Actions on the Objective

Just as with the ambush, the initiating volley of fire must physically and psychologically overwhelm the enemy force. Upon the initiating shot, every member of the patrol immediately opens fire on the objective regardless of whether they have a target. Failure to immediately suppress the enemy means failure. If the enemy gains the initiative, the patrol will likely be destroyed.

1. After effectively devastating the objective with a heavy volume of fire, the PL gives a designated signal to lift or shift fire. A common misconception is that the term "lift or shift" fire actually means "cease fire."

    Shifting fire means the support team's direction of fire shifts left or right to suppress enemy fleeing or reinforcing. If the coordination of elements does not permit a shifting of fire to be done safely, **lifting** fire means the support team fires harmlessly, well over everyone's heads.

The support team takes position after the security team gets into place. Because the support team carries heavy, crew-served weapons, more time must be allotted for their movement. Once in position, the support team signals the patrol leader.

The assault team moves into position last, after the support team is set. The assault team is lightly armed. It is responsible for closing the last few meters with the enemy. After the support team shifts fire, the assault team sweeps the objective.

Why? Because the effect of the support team's incredible volume of fire momentarily paralyzes the enemy's effort to fight back. A cease-fire, on the other hand, gives the enemy the impression that the attack has stalled. The enemy is more likely to detect and engage the lightly armed assault team. So, the answer is to either lift or shift fire, but do not cease fire until an appropriate time!

2. The assault team begins their choreographed attack across the objective. The assault team crosses the objective in pre-arranged buddy teams and

- Double-taps all enemy combatants (Shooting non-combatants is bad manners.)
- Secures the far side of the objective
- Conducts the sub-tasks of the specialty teams

3. Once the specialty teams are finished with the assigned tasks, the assault team leader gives the PL signals they are finished and ready to move.
4. The PL gives three designated signals. The first notifies the assault team to fall back through the release point to the ORP. The second notifies the support team to do the same. The third signal notifies the security team to fall back via their designated route to the ORP.

5. In the ORP, subordinate leaders reconsolidate and reorganize the patrol, accounting for all members and equipment. All crew-served weapons and priority equipment are reassigned if the operators have become casualties. Water and ammunition are redistributed.
6. The patrol falls back to a pre-designated position, usually one terrain feature back from the ORP. The patrol stops to disseminate all information and PIR regarding the raid among every patrol member prior to returning to the FEBA.

Raids happen for a multitude of reasons—most commonly to seize or destroy enemy assets, collect valuable information, or rescue personnel aligned with the patrol's cause.

The raid is a crowning achievement for any combat unit. It involves crossing that fine line between conventional warfare and the missions of the world's elite special force units. It is the stuff of brilliant tacticians and historic tales of success.

Patrols cannot conduct raids "on the fly." Of the hundreds of exhaustively planned and rehearsed raids assigned to three Allied airborne divisions dropped from the sky into France on the night of June 5, 1944, only one platoon accomplished its mission on time. That's right, only one! Good intelligence, special equipment, thorough rehearsals, and brilliant leadership are the only hope for a successful raid. Impromptu bravado will never do.

MAP AND UNIT SYMBOLS

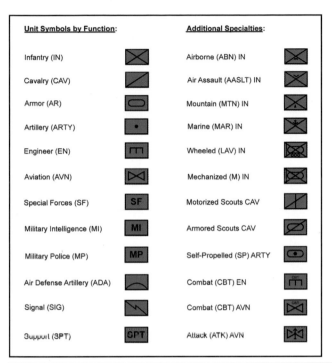

Unit Symbols by Function:

Infantry (IN)	
Cavalry (CAV)	
Armor (AR)	
Artillery (ARTY)	
Engineer (EN)	
Aviation (AVN)	
Special Forces (SF)	SF
Military Intelligence (MI)	MI
Military Police (MP)	MP
Air Defense Artillery (ADA)	
Signal (SIG)	
Support (SPT)	SPT

Additional Specialties:

Airborne (ABN) IN	
Air Assault (AASLT) IN	
Mountain (MTN) IN	
Marine (MAR) IN	
Wheeled (LAV) IN	
Mechanized (M) IN	
Motorized Scouts CAV	
Armored Scouts CAV	
Self-Propelled (SP) ARTY	
Combat (CBT) EN	
Combat (CBT) AVN	
Attack (ATK) AVN	

Left: The first step in using symbols to represent units is to understand who is being represented and what their capabilities and specialties are. This gives the commander and battle staff a better picture of how they can/should array their forces—that is, by capability. Additionally, a unit number identifier or name is often written to the lower right-hand side of the symbol.

Below: The next step is to grasp the symbols representing obstacles, actions, or even individual troops or crews. Using these graphics, the commander or battle staff can array their own resources, as well as better understand the enemy's resources.

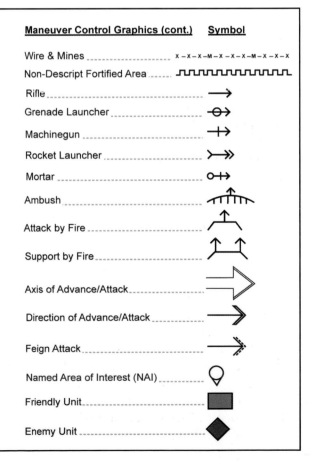

Unit	No. of Troops	Symbol
Fire team	4	○
Squad	9	•
Section	20	••
Platoon	30	•••
Company	120	I
Battalion	700	II
Regiment	2,000	III
Brigade	3,500	X
Division	18,000	XX
Corps	70,000	XXX

Maneuver Control Graphics   Symbol

Forward Line of Troops (FLOT)	
Forward Edge of Battle Area (FEBA)	
Wire Obstacle	
Minefield	

Maneuver Control Graphics (cont.)   Symbol

Wire & Mines	X – X – X – M – X – X – M – X – X – X
Non-Descript Fortified Area	
Rifle	
Grenade Launcher	
Machinegun	
Rocket Launcher	
Mortar	
Ambush	
Attack by Fire	
Support by Fire	
Axis of Advance/Attack	
Direction of Advance/Attack	
Feign Attack	
Named Area of Interest (NAI)	
Friendly Unit	
Enemy Unit	

GLOSSARY

AA, *Assembly Area,* noun: A location behind the FLOT where a unit waits pending further action.

AAR, *After-Action Review,* noun: 1. The reviewing process after a mission's end in which the component teams attempt to understand the sequence of the mission and learn from the cause-and-effect circumstances.
2. The plan; the performance; the issues; the fix.

AO, *Area of Operations,* noun: A geographical region marked by a boundary and assigned to a given unit to conduct operations.

APL, *Assistant Patrol Leader,* noun: The second-highest position within a patrol. Assists the primary patrol leader in carrying out tasks and responsibilities related to the mission.

Assault Position, noun: The last covered and concealed position *before* the OBJ, where the attacking force can finalize preparations and synchronize with coordinating units. The assault position is similar to the ORP except a patrol will return to an ORP after actions on the objective, and so it must be defended. The attacking force will *not* return to an assault position, therefore, no troops are left behind to defend it.

Assault Team, noun: An element of a larger force designated to assault across the enemy objective area. This team typically emphasizes maneuver and may carry lighter weapon systems than the support team.

Attack by Fire, verb: To fire at an enemy target or engagement area from a stationary position.

Attack Position, noun: The last position an offensive force occupies *before* crossing the LD; similar to the AA, but whereas the AA can be occupied for considerable lengths of time, the attack position is used to synchronize with adjacent units and to form the order of march. (Caution: Not the same as "assault position.")

Axis of Advance, noun: A line of advance assigned for purposes of control, typically involving left and right limits along an identifiable terrain feature, or a sequential series of locations.

Back Brief, noun: A process after the OPORD in which patrol members take part in a question-and-answer period to restate the mission in concise terms.

Battle, noun: The larger military fight, typically made up of a series of engagements over a given period of time.

Battle Drill, noun: A collective action or reaction, initiated by minimal orders, to a specific situation that does not allow enough time to assess and implement a decision-making process.

Battlespace, noun: A modern battlefield that takes into consideration all three dimensions of surface, subsurface, and atmosphere where opponents attempt to dominate and defeat each other using the maximum ranges and capabilities of their combat systems.

BLUFOR, *Blue Forces,* noun: Friendly forces during training exercises and scenario gaming that are indicated with blue, rectangular icons on a map.

Bound, verb: To move as an individual or team from one covered position to the next.

Break in Contact, noun: An unintentional incident resulting from a single formation breaking into two separate formations. Communication must be re-established between the two elements in order to continue the mission.

Brevity Code, noun: Short code words, typically one word per meaning, having no direct connotation to the message they encrypt. Example: "Buick" meaning "Established ORP."

C4ISR, *Command, Control, Communication, Computers, Intelligence, Surveillance, Reconnaissance,* noun: Regarding those systems that give the commander a better picture of the operating environment—particularly enemy activity—and better control over troop movement. Sometimes called C2, C3, or C4I in abbreviated form.

Call Signs, noun: Short codes identifying the calling and receiving stations for radio transmissions.

CCIR, *Commander's Critical Information Requirements,* noun: Information the commander needs to know to plan and conduct the mission. The commander uses CCIR to delineate the FFIR and PIR, and thereby identifies NAI.

CEOI, *Communications-Electronic Operating Instructions* (formerly *Counter-Encrypting Operations and Intelligence*), noun: A code book or document of highly sensitive information that includes the call signs, radio frequencies, passwords, and encrypting codes for mission-essential radio procedures. See also SOI.

Choke Point, noun: An area of restricted movement, usually due to terrain limitations.

Clock Method, concept: Determining a direction wherein twelve o'clock is the dead-ahead position; three o'clock is to the right of the formation; nine o'clock is to the left of the formation; and six o'clock is to the rear of the formation.

CO, *Commanding Officer,* noun: The officer in charge of a given military unit who is responsible for planning, leading, and directing troops through subordinate leaders.

COA, *Course of Action,* noun: A plan that directly impacts the accomplishment of the mission.

COE, *Common Operating Environment,* noun: Offers the commander a familiarization with the operating environment so the commander may focus on the crisis at hand; makes ample use of C4ISR.

Combat Power, noun: The total means of resources, such as troops, supplies, and weapon systems, forming the destructive force used against the enemy.

Commander's Intent, noun: The commander's concise expression of (1) the purpose of the operation, (2) the key tasks that must be achieved to complete the missions, and (3) a vision of how the end-state physically looks and/or functions.

Concealment, noun: Any materials or situation, such as darkness, which may camouflage an individual's position or movement from visible detection.

Contact, verb: 1. To see, hear, or otherwise detect the enemy. noun: 2. Firsthand knowledge of the location or direction of an enemy force.

Contingency Plan, noun: Instructions given by a leader when splitting the patrol into two or more elements and detailing what each party will do in specific situations.

CP, *Command Post,* noun: The physical location where the command team conducts its activities within a static position.

Cover, noun: Any obstacle offering protection from direct or indirect hostile fire that camouflages an individual's position from visual detection.

Culmination, noun: A situation in which the combat power of the offensive force is no longer effective against the defending enemy. Conversely, a situation in which the combat power of the defense can no longer repel an attacking enemy.

Decisive Operation/Action noun: An engagement in which both opponents are fully committed, and an extraction from the fight is unlikely. A battle fought to a conclusion with one side or the other yielding.

Defeat in Detail, noun: A battle in which attacking forces fix and destroy a smaller element of the enemy while the enemy is unable to coordinate with adjacent units for help. After this unit is destroyed or captured, the attacking forces continue this sequence of fix and destroy until all or most of the enemy has been defeated.

Direction of Attack, noun: A specific direction for an attacking force that does not permit the bypassing of obstacles or other enemy troops. Often this is assigned to an identifiable terrain feature or route.

Displace, verb: To move laterally or rearward with regard to the enemy position to gain a better vantage point. Displacement is commonly used in the Break Contact battle drill and retrograde defensive operations.

Disrupt, verb: To impair or destroy the enemy's ability to communicate, coordinate, and synchronize their combat power.

Drag Man, noun: The last man in the order of march; the troop at the end of the formation whose duty it is to maintain rear security and be certain that no other member of the patrol falls behind.

EA, *Engagement Area*, noun: The designated location to employ combat power to destroy the enemy.

EEFI, *Essential Elements of Friendly Information*, noun: The information the commander needs to hide from the enemy. Commanders must be cognizant of this information when developing the CCIR.

Element, noun: Any military unit, or even an unspecified part of a military unit.

Elusiveness, adjective: Having properties to avoid detection by the enemy either through stealth or mobility.

ENDEX, *End Exercise*, verb: To end all actions relating to the military exercise.

End State, noun: The desired situation when operations conclude.

Engagement, noun: A firefight; tactical skirmishes between opposing forces that may or may not have a conclusive result.

Engagement Priority, noun: A priority of enemy targets assigned either to specific weapon crews or to all friendly troops under specific conditions.

Enveloping Force, noun: A tactical maneuver in which a smaller friendly element moves around the enemy's main defenses (1) to disrupt the enemy operations while a larger element conducts an attack from another direction, or (2) to fix the enemy in their routes of withdrawal until the main attack is able to defeat the enemy in detail.

ERP, *En-route Rally Point*, noun: An easily identified point on the ground where a patrol may regroup if they become separated or defend if they need to fall back unexpectedly.

ETA, *Estimated Time of Arrival*, noun: This estimate is often used as part of a contingency plan, or to develop the plan for an OPORD.

ETD, *Estimated Time of Departure*, noun: An estimate used to plan time hacks for an OPORD.

Far Ambush, noun: A surprise attack on a moving or temporarily halted enemy target from a concealed position at a distance *farther* than hand-grenade range (i.e., >35 meters).

FEBA, *Forward Edge of Battle Area*, noun: An engagement area visible *beyond* the friendly FLOT.

Feign Attack, noun: A deceptive attack used to confuse the enemy about the location or time of the actual attack.

FFIR, *Friendly Force Information Requirements*, noun: Those identified conditions negatively or positively impacting the force's ability to achieve the mission. These considerations are delineated by the CCIR.

Fire Control Measures/Graphics, noun: The coordination of fire ensuring maximum effect on the enemy target and minimizing fratricide. Additionally, the graphic representation of this coordination as marked on a map.

Fix, verb: To prevent an enemy force from moving by maneuvering to a superior position and attacking by fire.

Flank, verb: To intentionally avoid the enemy's frontal fire by maneuvering left or right in search of an exposed enemy flank.

FLOT, *Forward Line of Troops*, noun: The line on a map or terrain model identifying the most forward friendly troops in any combat operation.

FRAGO, *Fragmentary Order*, noun: An abbreviated form of the OPORD, making adjustments to the original order without restating those sections that haven't changed.

Fratricide, (aka Friendly Fire), noun: Firing weapon systems with the intent of killing enemy troops but unintentionally killing or wounding your own troops instead.

FUC, *Forward Unit Commander*, noun: The commanding officer of the most forward friendly unit in a given operation.

GNDR, *Grenadier*, noun: A soldier whose responsibility includes employing grenades and grenade launchers to destroy hardened targets, break up enemy formations, or attack defilades with indirect fire.

Grazing Fire, noun: 1. Fire running approximately parallel to the ground, not raised more than one meter from the surface of the ground. 2. Automatic fire employed over flat, open terrain against massed targets and targets of opportunity.

HQ, *Headquarters*, noun: The physical location where the commander and staff of a larger unit (typically a battalion or higher) conduct activities within a static position.

IED, *Improvised Explosive Device*, noun: Less-than-conventional explosives used in mechanical ambushes; favorite tactic of guerilla fighters and terrorists.

IMT, *Individual Movement Techniques*, noun: A series of techniques used by the individual to move from one covered position to another while under enemy fire, offering the least exposure to the enemy's direct-fire systems. (Movements include the low crawl, high crawl, modified crawl, and rush.)

Kill Zone, noun: An engagement area, as in ambushes and raids, where combat power is concentrated to fix, isolate, and destroy an enemy force.

LACE, *Liquid, Ammunition, Casualties, and Equipment*, noun: Key considerations in the process of reconsolidation and reorganization during battle, including the care and evacuation of wounded, manning of key weapon and communication systems, and redistribution of ammunition and water among troops.

LD, *Line of Departure*, noun: The *first* phase line to be crossed at a designated time by troops initiating an offensive operation. (Also LOD.)

LOA, *Limit of Advance,* noun: The *last* phase line in an offensive operation that troops are *not* permitted to cross.

LZ, *Landing Zone,* noun: A suitable area designated for the landing of troops via helicopter; point of insertion.

MA, *Mechanical Ambush,* noun: A near ambush making use of anti-personnel and/or anti-armor land mines instead of troops with direct-fire weapons.

Mass, verb: To physically concentrate combat power by condensing resources into a smaller geographic area and focusing against a given target; one tenet of the Principles of War.

METT-TC, *Mission, Enemy, Terrain and weather, Time available, Troops available, and Civilians on the battlefield,* noun.

MG, *Machine Gun,* noun: A heavy-barreled weapon capable of firing rifle cartridges at fully automatic, cyclic rates of fire. Machine guns come in three general categories: light, medium, and heavy.

MGR, *Machine Gunner,* noun: A soldier whose responsibility includes employing a machine gun.

Mission, noun: An identified task and purpose clearly indicating the action to be taken and the reason action is necessary.

Movement Control Measures/Graphics, noun: The planning, routing, and scheduling of units and equipment toward an objective; the graphic representation of this coordination on a map.

MTC, *Movement to Contact,* noun: An offensive operation seeking to gain or regain enemy contact; used when the commander does not have enough information to conduct a deliberate attack.

NAI, *Named Areas of Interest,* noun: Identified locations on the ground where the commander requires specific information to be collected; dictated by the PIR.

Near Ambush, noun: A surprise attack on a moving or temporarily halted enemy target from a concealed position *within* hand-grenade range (i.e., <35 meters).

NLT, *No Later Than,* noun: A limit of time designating a deadline for an operation to either start or complete.

NVG, *Night Vision Goggles,* noun: Also, NOD and NVD for *Night Optic Devices* and *Night Vision Devices,* respectively. Night vision goggles, such as the popular PVS-7B model, use passive light technology for nighttime operations. Night optic device is the more encompassing term and includes passive light and infrared technology, but it also includes much simpler, cheaper devices like the high-power tactical weapon lights.

OBJ, *Objective,* noun: A location on the ground used to orient the operation, whether the operation is combative, logistical, or humanitarian.

OCOKA, *Observation, Cover and concealment, Obstacles, Key terrain, Avenues of approach,* noun: Tactical considerations for securing any static position, such as determining a location to establish a defensive line, ambush, patrol base, or ORP.

OPFOR, *Opposing Forces,* noun: The enemy forces during training exercises and scenario gaming; indicated by red, diamond icons on a map.

OP/LP, *Observation Post/Listening Post,* noun: The position forward of the FLOT from which security observations are made to alert the main body of the unit; appropriate communications are required.

OPORD, *Operation Order,* noun: 1. A directive issued by the commander to coordinate the execution of an operation. 2. A five-paragraph mission plan that includes:
1. Situation
2. Mission
3. Execution
4. Service and Support—U.S. Army (Administration and Logistics—USMC)
5. Command and Signal

Order of March, noun: A coordinating directive establishing where each individual or unit will line up in the patrol's formation.

ORP, *Objective Rally Point,* noun: A covered and concealed position three hundred meters or one terrain feature from the OBJ where final preparations are made prior to moving to the OBJ.

Overwatch, verb: To provide security through an attack by fire or the potential to effect such an attack.

PB, *Patrol Base,* noun: A temporary position providing 360-degree security through which an element may conduct a series of patrols; never used more than twenty-four hours at a time.

PIR, *Priority Information Requirements,* noun: Information needed about the enemy force; delineated by the CCIR.

PL, 1. *Patrol Leader,* noun. 2. *Phase Line,* noun.

Plunging Fire, noun: 1. The method of firing a weapon system in reference to the ground. 2. Direct fire plunging down from high angles or at the maximum effective range of the weapon so the direct fire has a considerable arch.

Point Man, noun: 1. The first man in the order of march. 2. The troop at the front of the formation whose is responsible for navigating while disclosing the patrol's position or leading the patrol into an ambush, minefield, or fall from a cliff.

Principles of War, concept: 1. The tenets of warfare used by military leaders to plan and execute combat operations. 2. Using the pneumonic device MOSS-MOUSE: Mass, Objective, Surprise, Security, Maneuver, Offensive, Unity of command, Simplicity, and Economy of force.

PZ, *Pickup Zone,* noun: 1. A suitable area designated for the loading of troops, casualties, and POWs via helicopter during or after combat missions. 2. A point of extraction.

R&S Patrol, *Reconnaissance and Security Patrol,* noun: An information-gathering patrol conducted within the local area in front of or around a designated defensive posture.

Rally Point, noun: A designated position for the patrol to regroup in the event it comes in contact with an overwhelming enemy force in the near future. See also ERP, ORP.

Release Point, noun: 1. The point during a mission when the patrol leader releases authority to subordinate element leaders. 2. The physical location where the patrol will part into separate teams to achieve mission goals.

Reserve Force, noun: A body of troops intentionally withheld from action at the onset of an operation or engagement. This element is available for decisive action or to return the momentum to an offensive operation.

RFL, *Restrictive Fire Line,* noun: The line on the map between two converging friendly forces prohibiting firing of weapons; ideally follows a recognizable terrain feature.

RM, *Rifleman,* noun: A soldier whose responsibility includes employing a rifle, a bayonet, and an assortment of explosives or missiles to close with, engage, and defeat an enemy in all terrain, weather, and light conditions.

ROE, *Rules Of Engagement*, noun: A commander's directive delineating the conditions and limitations under which troops will initiate engagement and/or continue engagement with a specified threat.

RTO, *Radio Telephone Operator*, noun: 1. A soldier whose responsibilities include the operation of radios and field phones, as well as encrypting and decrypting messages. 2. Any rifleman with a radio.

Screening Force, noun: The element providing security and early warning to the main body of the unit.

Sector of Fire, noun: An engagement area assigned to an individual, weapons crew, or unit in which enemy targets will be engaged according to stated or implied conditions and priorities.

Sector Sketch, noun: A hand-drawn or otherwise graphically represented overview of a unit's defensive measures, including the location of fighting positions, interlocked sectors of fire, wire and mine obstacles, OP/LP, CP, defilades, grazing fire, TRP, maximum engagement of weapons, alternate fighting positions, and tie-ins with adjacent friendly elements.

Shaping Operation/Action, noun: An engagement creating conditions for success of a decisive operation; operations and actions include: reconnaissance, screening patrols, multiple simultaneous attacks to disrupt the enemy, feign attacks to compel the enemy's reserves, seizing of advantages in terrain, and fixing or delaying of enemy forces.

Shift Fire, verb: To adjust the principal direction of fire to avoid shooting friendly forces who are assaulting a kill zone, to engage an enemy fleeing from a kill zone, and to keep enemy troops from reinforcing an enemy target within a kill zone.

SITREP, *Situation Report*, noun: A brief report in which the patrol leader relays mission-essential information to higher command. This helps command visualize the mission as it unfolds and allows them to amend the mission with frag-Os to achieve the mission goals.

Situational Awareness, noun: Responsiveness to an environment and constantly evolving situation relating to strengths, weaknesses, opportunities, and threats (SWOT).

SL, *Squad Leader*, noun: A non-commissioned officer leading a squad as either an independent unit or as part of a larger military unit; leads, supervises, and directs two or three fireteam leaders and reports to the platoon sergeant and/or platoon leader.

SMG, *Sub-Machine Gun*, noun: A light-barreled weapon capable of firing pistol cartridges at fully automatic, cyclic rates of fire.

SOI, *Signal Operating Instructions*, noun: A code book or document of highly sensitive information including call signs, radio frequencies, and passwords for mission-essential radio procedures. See also CEOI.

SOP, *Standard Operating Procedure*, noun: Tasks conducted often enough to merit standard procedure so that the execution becomes second nature and all team members know how to respond without asking for guidance.

SP, *Start Point*, noun: The initial location along the route of march where each unit falls under command of that unit's designated leader.

Standoff Weaponry/Capability, noun: The classification of combat weapon systems that are highly mobile and have the capability to be employed at distances negating enemy countermeasures. Historical examples include but are not limited to: the longbow, artillery and mortars, the torpedo, booby-traps, and IED (improvised explosive devices).

SUC, *Supporting Unit Commander*, noun: The commanding officer of any supporting friendly unit within a given operation.

Support by Fire, verb: To provide suppressive fire from a static position against an enemy target in support of another maneuvering friendly unit.

Support Team, noun: The element tasked to maneuver to a position providing maximum advantage for supporting fire.

Suppressive Fire, noun: Fire directed against an opponent seeking to temporarily degrade the enemy's ability to employ their own weapon systems.

Surprise, verb: To attack without warning or to catch an opponent unaware, leaving the enemy without time or resources to react.

Sustaining Operation/Action, noun: Actions along lines of communication enabling momentum and freedom of maneuver for decisive and shaping operations.

SWOT, *Strengths, Weaknesses, Opportunities, and Threats*, noun: Principal considerations for the assessment of an environment pertaining to situational awareness.

Terrain Model, (aka Sand Table), noun: A three-dimensional representation of terrain used to orient troops to their OBJ.

TL, *Fireteam Leader*, noun: Also ATL, BTL, CTL for *Alpha Team Leader*, *Bravo Team Leader*, and *Charlie Team Leader*, respectively. A non-commissioned officer leading a fireteam as either an independent unit or as part of a larger military unit.

TLP, *Troop Leading Procedures*, noun: The process of leading, managing, directing, and supervising troops through the development and implementation of the mission orders. The process includes: (1) Receive the mission, (2) Issue a WARNO, (3) Make a tentative plan, (4) Begin movement, (5) Reconnoiter, (6) Complete the plan, (7) Issue an OPORD, (8) Supervise and refine the mission.

TRP, *Target Reference Point*, noun: An easily recognized location on the ground used to initiate, adjust, and control fire within an engagement area.

Vanguard, noun: Troops or an element moving ahead of the main body of the patrol for the purpose of security.

VOA ,*Violence of Action*, concept: The notion that violent action is a force multiplier that momentarily stuns the enemy and, thereby, accelerates the forward momentum of an engagement.

WARNO, *Warning Order*, noun: An order providing advanced notice of an impending OPORD; allows leaders to begin TLP and troops to prepare for the mission.

Weapon Safety Posture, concept: A system of safety conditions regarding the relative danger from the enemy, reconciled with the danger of fratricide. Weapon safety postures can be specific to a given weapon system or can apply generally to all troops. Also known as "Weapon Readiness Conditions," the following is a common example:
Condition 1: Magazine loaded, a round *is* chambered, weapon on safe.
Condition 2: Magazine loaded, *no* round is chambered, weapon on safe.
Condition 3: Weapon unloaded, loaded magazines in pouches.

XO, *Executive Officer*, noun: The officer assigned as second-in-command of any military unit at the company level or higher.

INDEX